American Animated Films:
The Silent Era, 1897–1929

American Animated Films: The Silent Era, 1897–1929

by

Denis Gifford

McFarland & Company, Inc., Publishers
Jefferson, North Carolina, and London

for

FELIX THE CAT

not forgetting his masters,

PAT SULLIVAN

and especially

OTTO MESSMER

British Library Cataloguing-in-Publication data are available

Library of Congress Cataloguing-in-Publication Data

Gifford, Denis.
    American animated films : the silent era, 1897–1929 / Denis
Gifford.
    Includes indexes.
    ISBN 0-89950-460-4 (lib. bdg. : 50# alk. paper) ∞
    1. Animated films—United States—Catalogs.   2. Silent films—
United States—Catalogs. I. Title.
NC1766.U5G54   1990
016.79143′75′097309041—dc20   89-43649
                                                           CIP

Manufactured in the United States of America

McFarland & Company, Inc., Publishers
  Box 611, Jefferson, North Carolina 28640

Contents

Introduction

This book represents the first attempt to catalogue animated films made in the United States of America during the silent era. This era ran from the earliest experiments by the English-born newspaper cartoonist James Stuart Blackton at the Edison "Black Maria" Studio in April 1897, to the successful premiere of Walter Elias Disney's soundtrack-synchronized *Steamboat Willie* at the Colony Theatre, New York, on 18 November 1928. The period is not quite so precisely defined as that, however. Some evidence points to Blackton making his first experimental film in August 1896, while there were earlier experiments with synchronized soundtracks before *Steamboat Willie* and at least a year of continuing silent cartoon production after.

This book forms a companion volume to my earlier *British Animated Films, 1895–1985* (McFarland, 1987), but because of the far greater output of American production, takes the story only as far as the introduction of sound. This break-off represents more than convenience, however: Sound proved to be a watershed as much in animated cartoon films as it did in feature films. Perhaps more so, as music and comical effects gave a whole new dimension to cartoons, lifting them out of program filler fodder to virtual star status and a true "added attraction" to the cinema bill.

The arrangement of the films in this book is chronological within series. That is, since it proved impractical to list every film as a separate entry in its own right, I have arranged them under the names of the series in which the majority of the films were produced, and the series are listed chronologically according to their earliest entries. Where the films do not have a regular character or hero represented in a series title, they are listed under their producer or animator, e.g. *Blackton Cartoons*, or the title of the film series in which they were included as a segment or episode, e.g. *Universal Animated Weekly*. (Parenthetically it is worth mentioning here that the title of this regular newsreel produced by the Universal Manufacturing Company uses the word "animated" in its then current sense of "animated pictures," an alternative term for "moving pictures," and does not imply a weekly release of animated cartoons. The title has caused some confusion for amateur historians of the medium.) Through the chronological arrangement, this book presents the evolution of American animation just as it originally unfolded. Individual titles can be easily tracked through the alphabetical index. The work of individuals in the field can also be tracked via a separate alphabetical index of names. All numbers given in the indexes are entry numbers, not page numbers.

The evolution of the American animated film follows a track surprisingly parallel to that of the British cartoon. It begins with the simple recording on film of a cartoonist in action: the three one-minute kinetoscope films made in 1896 and 1897 of J. Stuart Blackton, a newspaper cartoonist who gave "lightning cartoon" entertainments to audiences, exactly echo the four one-minute films made in 1895 and 1896 of Tom Merry (William Machin), also a newspaper cartoonist. Interestingly, while Blackton was filmed in New York, and Merry was filmed in London, both cartoonists were British. At roughly the same time, Georges Méliès, the French pioneer producer, was filming another lightning cartoonist in his Paris studio. Blackton followed Méliès by moving into film production, cofounding the Vitagraph Corporation of America and becoming the first giant all-round talent in American cinema, producing, directing, scripting, performing, and devising special effects. Small wonder, perhaps, that cartooning, even of the animated variety, formed a decreasing element of his work load. However, Blackton is the undoubted founding father of the animated cartoon, developing his elementary "chalk-talk" act as recorded for Edison in *The Enchanted Drawing* (November 1900), in which he is seen making sketches that come alive through photographic trickery, through *Humorous Phases of Funny Faces* (April 1906) and, a year later, *Lightning Sketches*. Oddly, while the French animator Emile Cohl claimed to have learned animation through the close study of Blackton's work, he took those lessons from Blackton's stop-frame animation of objects in *The Haunted Hotel* (March 1907), rather than through any of his cartoon films.

Emile Cohl (Courtet), a comic strip artist who founded the French animated cartoon industry with his *Fantasmagorie* (1908), would come to America in late 1912 to make a weekly topical or political cartoon item for the French-based weekly newsreel, *Eclair Journal*. Meanwhile, the American strip cartoonist Winsor McCay, creator of the popular Sunday newspaper series "Little Nemo in Slumberland," experimented with bringing his character to life on the cinema screen. In this he was assisted by J. Stuart Blackton, who produced and released the film through his Vitagraph Company in April 1911. Where Blackton had filmed himself working in continuity, stopping the camera while he drew additions to his cartoons on a board, McCay devised a system of making a series of separate drawings on cards, each depicting a continuity of movement from its predecessor, each photographed a frame at a time by the movie camera. McCay also linked with Blackton and the early pioneers by being a practicing chalk-talker. He took his films into the variety theatres and used them as part of his act. Later, live-action footage was added so that the cartoon sequences could be released to the cinemas. McCay also devised a way to repeat his drawings in cycles, cutting down drawing time — a technique still employed by the producers of cartoons for television.

It was perhaps natural affinity that linked comic strip to animation in America. McCay had animated his own "Little Nemo," and George McManus, creator of "The Newlyweds" of *The New York World*, was included in the live-action sequences. Cohl, animating the weekly cartoon item for *Eclair Journal*, was given the additional task of animating the McManus characters for an *Eclair* series of their own. Beginning in January 1913 with *When He Wants a Dog He Wants a Dog*, a run of fifteen "Newlyweds" (or "Snookums") films was produced, making up the first genuine cartoon film series. Hot on Baby Snookums' heels came Harry Conway Fisher, better known as "Bud," with a series based on his popular daily paper heroes, "Mutt and Jeff." This comic pair had already been filmed as a sequence of still drawings for the newsreel *Pathé's Weekly*, and now they formed an animated "comic supplement." Fisher soon set up his own production company, and with the genius Charles Bowers directing the animation, launched what would become the longest run of any cartoon series, 288 being listed in this book with more yet to be traced! These are also the oldest animated cartoons still circulated, several having been colorized and synchronized for video release.

John Randolph Bray has rightly been dubbed "the Henry Ford of animation" by Donald Crafton in his book *Before Mickey* (Massachusetts Institute of Technology, 1982). Another graduate from the comic strip academy (his "Johnny and the Teddy Bears" ran weekly in *Judge* magazine from 1907), Bray saw McCay give his animated chalk-talk show and was inspired to make his own cartoons move. Quickly realizing the difficulty of drawing sufficient separate cartoons to fill a thousand feet of film (the length of a single reel, the basic unit of release), he topped and tailed his first effort with live action of himself making a drawing of a dachshund and falling asleep at the drawing-board. Then the cartoon dog came to life, until the artist's wife (Margaret Bray) awakened him. Pathé saw the film and wanted a regular monthly release. Even with live action sequences, the amount of drawing required proved impossible, so Bray devised a time-saving method. He had the unchanging section of each scene or sequence printed on sheets of tracing paper, so that only the moving figures needed to be redrawn. Bray's first patent, number 1107193, laid the foundation of the American animation industry. Five months after his first attempt, Bray was launching the first adventure of his own regular hero, *Colonel Heeza Liar* (November 1913), and would soon be forced to abandon drawing for running the world's first film factory to specialize in animation of all kinds.

The comic strip connection continued with the entry of press baron William Randolph Hearst into the movie business via his International Film Service and its twice-weekly newsreel, *The Hearst-Vitagraph News Pictorial.* Beginning in a small way with a regular "comic supplement" item animated from Tom Powers' newspaper strip, "Phables" (December 1915), within months Hearst's studio was producing cartoon releases in their own right, adapted from highly popular syndicated Sunday strips: Opper's "Maud the Mule" and "Happy Hooligan," Herriman's "Krazy Kat," Hoban's "Jerry on the Job," McManus' "Bringing Up Father," and others. Hearst's brilliance in picking the right man for the job is shown in his selection of a young but experienced animator, Gregory La Cava, as his animation production chief. La Cava not only organized each series with its own autonomous crew, he devised the "hosepipe" style of drawing unjointed limbs, simplifying the animation of humans and animals with one inspired swoop. After Hearst closed his animation studio in July 1918, La Cava went on to become a top comedy director of Hollywood movies.

There are too many major talents in our chosen era to detail here; their work will be found listed in the body of this book. But mention must be made of Earl Hurd, the first to patent the "cel" process (drawing part of each frame on transparent celluloid, separating moving parts from static backgrounds), and the creator of the long-running *Bobby Bumps* series; Paul Terry, who from a shaky start would run his *Farmer Al Falfa* from silence through sound, color and ultimately television via his *Terrytoons;* Pat Sullivan, an Australian comic artist, whose *Sammie Johnsin* series about a little black boy would lead to the creation, aided by Otto Messmer, of a little black cat, *Felix,* the first international star of animated cartoons; the zany offbeat talent of Milt Gross, who would continue to switch from animation to the comic page through quite a career; the technical virtuosity of Max Fleischer, who would dress his brother Dave as a clown and convert the films of him into cartoon drawings via his invention, the rotoscope, still used in the industry 70 years after the first *Out of the Inkwell;* and Walt Disney who, in collaboration with his friend and fellow cartoonist, Ubbe Iwerks, would eventually write finis to our era with *Mickey Mouse.*

My grateful thanks are due to Patrick J. Sheehan, Reference Librarian (Motion Picture Section) of the Library of Congress, Washington, D.C., for time and trouble taken in researching on my behalf. Also to Guy Coté of La Cinémathèque Canadienne, and Leonard Maltin, then of *Film Fan Monthly:* both provided information unavailable in England. This project was begun in 1967, so my thanks and apologies to those others who helped but whose names have been mislaid in the interim. Finally, thanks to David Coates for his help on the indexes.

Additional information and corrections will be gratefully received by the author in care of the publisher.

How to Use This Book

Each film in this book is listed under the title of the series in which it was an entry. The series titles are listed in chronological order, and the individual films are also in chronological order within each series. Chronology is determined by release dates (where known) or copyright dates.

Each series has been assigned an entry number; individual films within the series have subentry numbers. The title and name indexes at the back of the book locate films via these entry and subentry numbers.

Some titles appear under more than one series heading, as many of the main series of the period grouped several minor series under their larger umbrellas.

Entries are presented according to the following format:

92.[1] *Felix the Cat*[2]

Pat Sullivan Comics[3]
Producer/Director: Pat Sullivan[4]
Animation: Otto Messmer, Raoul Barré, Dana Parker, Hal Walker, Al Eugster, Jack Boyle, George Cannata, Tom Byrne, Alfred Thurber[5]

Paramount Magazine[6]
Distributor: Paramount[7]

1920[8]

(1)[9]   March 28[10]   *Feline Follies*[11] (650)[12]

(2)   April 18   (title unknown)[13]
continued in *Paramount Cartoons*[14]
continued as Winkler Productions[15]

NB:[16]

     1. entry number
     2. title of series; includes alternate titles (aka) and British titles (GB), where known to exist
     3. production company
     4. production credits
     5. animation credits for the series
     6. film titles appearing below this notation were included as items in or segments of a series by this differing title
     7. distributor (refers to all films below this notation, until another distributor is noted)
     8. year
     9. subentry number
     10. month and day of release
     11. title of film or series episode
     12. length of film, in feet
     13. indicates that no title has been traced for release of this date
     14. change of series within which cartoon is an item (refers to all films below this notation, until another series title is noted)
     15. indicates change of production company or distributor
     16. *nota bene:* any special comment worth noting

The abbreviation "aka" indicates "also known as," an alternative title. The abbreviation "GB" indicates the title under which the film was released in Great Britain.

The Films

1. Blackton Cartoons

aka: *Blackman Cartoons*
Thomas A. Edison Kinetoscope
Drawn by James Stuart Blackton

1897
- **(1)** April   *Humorous Cartoon* (150)
- **(2)** April   *Political Cartoon* (150)
- **(3)** April   *Sketching Mr. Edison* (150)

NB: J. Stuart Blackton filmed performing his "lightning cartoonist" act. Not animated cartoons, but the earliest American films of a cartoonist. May have been filmed August 1896.

2. Vitagraph Cartoons

Vitagraph Corporation
Producer/Director/Story/Animation/Actor: J. Stuart Blackton
Combined live action and animation.

1900
- **(1)** Nov. 16   *The Enchanted Drawing*

1906
- **(2)** April 16   *Humorous Phases of Funny Faces* (225)

1907
- **(3)** July 15   *Lightning Sketches* (600)

1

1909

   (4)   July 17   *The Magic Fountain Pen* (475)

3.   *Winsor McCay Cartoons*

McCay
Producer/Director/Story/Animation: Winsor McCay

1911

   (1)   April 8   *Winsor McCay* (650)
                     GB: *Winsor McCay and His Animated Comics*
                     aka: *Winsor McCay Makes His Cartoons Move*
                           Winsor McCay Explains His Moving Cartoons to John Bunny
                           Little Nemo
                     Vitagraph Film Corp.
                     Director (live action): J. Stuart Blackton
                     Photography (live action): Walter Arthur
                     Actors: Winsor McCay, John Bunny, George McManus
                     Based on the comic strip "Little Nemo in Slumberland."

1912

   (2)   Jan.   *The Story of a Mosquito* (541)
                     GB: *The Hungry Mosquito*
                     Reissue: *Winsor McCay and His Jersey Skeeters*
                     aka: *How a Mosquito Operates*
                     Distributor: Vitagraph
                     Actors: Winsor McCay, Miss McCay
                     Based on the comic strip "The Dreams of the Rarebit Fiend."

1914

   (3)   Sept. 15   *Gertie*
                     aka: *Gertie the Dinosaurus*
                           Gertie the Dinosaur
                           Gertie the Trained Dinosaur
                     Distributor: Box Office Attractions

Actors: Winsor McCay, George McManus, Roy
McCardell
(NB: Used as part of McCay's vaudeville act,
and lengthened with live action footage for
theatrical release)
Gertie the Dinosaur
Director/Animation: John R. Bray
Scenario: Frederick Melville
(NB: It is not known whether this second ver-
sion is an "official" remake of McCay's film,
or a pirated version.)

1918

(4)   May 18   *The Sinking of the Lusitania* (900)
Distributor: Jewel Productions/Universal
Assistant: John A. Fitzsimmons, Apthorp
Adams

4. *Universal Animated Weekly*

Universal Pictures
Production: Carl Laemmle
Director/Story/Animation: Hy (Henry) Mayer (and others)
"Topical Cartoon"—cartoon sequence included in weekly news-
reel

1912–1918

Untitled cartoon series commencing October 1,
1912, and ending December 1, 1918.

5. *The Gaumont Weekly*

Gaumont Co.
Topical cartoon sequence included in weekly newsreel.

1912

(1)   Nov. 13   No. 36: *Waiting for the Robert E. Lee*
(2)   Nov. 27   No. 38: *The War News in Constantinople*
(3)   Dec. 4   No. 39: *The Struggle Between Producer and
Consumer*

(4) Dec. 18 No. 41: *The Fate of the Foxes*

1913
(5) Jan. 15 No. 45: *What a Fall, Oh My Countrymen*

6. *Eclair Journal*

Eclair Co.
Director/Story/Animation: Emile Cohl
Animated cartoon items in a weekly newsreel.

1913
(1)	Jan.	*War in Turkey*
(2)	Jan.	*Castro in New York*
(3)	Jan.	*Rockefeller*
(4)	Jan.	*Confidence*
(5)	Feb.	*Milk*
(6)	Feb.	*Coal*
(7)	Feb.	*The Subway*
(8)	Feb.	*Graft*
(9)	March	*The Two Presidents*
(10)	March	*The Auto*
(11)	March	*Wilson and the Broom*
(12)	March	*The Police Women*
(13)	March	*Wilson and the Hats*
(14)	March	*Poker*
(15)	March	*Gaynor and the Night Clubs*
(16)	March	*Universal Trade Marks*
(17)	April	*Wilson and the Tariffs*
(18)	April	*The Masquerade*
(19)	April	*The Brand of California*
(20)	May	*The Safety Pin*
(21)	May	*The Two Suffragettes*
(22)	May	*The Mosquito*
(23)	May	*The Red Balloons*
(24)	June	*The Cubists*
(25)	June	*Uncle Sam and His Suit*
(26)	June	*The Polo Boat*
(27)	June	*The Artist*

(28) July   *Wilson's Row Row*
(29) Aug.   *The Hat*
(30) Aug.   *Thaw and the Lasso*
(31) Aug.   *Bryant and the Speeches*
(32) Sept.   *Thaw and the Spider*
(33) Nov.   *Exhibition of Caricatures*
(34) Dec.   *Pickup Is a Sportsman*

1914

(35) Jan.   *The Bath*
(36) Jan.   *The Future Revealed by the Lines of the Feet*
(37) Nov.   *The Social Group*
(38)   *The Greedy Neighbor*
(39)   *What They Eat*
(40)   *The Anti-Neurasthenic Trumpet*
(41)   *His Ancestors*
(42)   *Serbia's Card*
(43)   *The Terrible Scrap of Paper*

7. *The Newlyweds*

aka: *Their Only Child*
aka: *Snookums*
Eclair Films
Director/Animation: Emile Cohl
From the comic strip by George McManus.

1913

(1) Jan. 18   *When He Wants a Dog He Wants a Dog*
(2) March 15   *Business Must Not Interfere*
(3) March 29   *He Wants What He Wants When He Wants It*
(4) April 20   *Poor Little Chap He Was Only Dreaming*
(5) May 18   *He Loves to Watch the Flight of Time*
(6) June 1   *He Ruins His Family's Reputation*
(7) June 15   *He Slept Well*
(8) June 19   *He Was Not Ill Only Unhappy*
(9) July 13   *It Is Hard to Please Him but It Is Worth It*
(10) July 27   *He Poses for His Portrait*
             GB: *Snookums' Portrait*

(11) Oct. 19 *He Loves to Be Amused*
(12) Dec. 14 *He Likes Things Upside Down*

1914
(13) Jan. 17 *He Does Not Care to Be Photographed*
(14) Feb.   *He Never Objects to Noise*
(15) Feb.   *He Only Wanted to Play with Dodo*

8. *Mutt and Jeff*

Pathé Frères Co.
Based on the comic strip by Harry "Bud" Fisher.
In *Pathé's Weekly*
"Comic supplement" to a weekly newsreel.

1913
(1)   Feb. 10   *Mutt and Jeff*
(2)   Feb. 17   *Mutt and Jeff*
(3)   Feb. 24   *Mutt and Jeff*
(4)   March 3   *Mutt and Jeff at Sea*
(5)   March 10 *Mutt and Jeff at Sea (continued)*
(6)   March 17 *Mutt and Jeff in Constantinople*
(7)   March 24 *The Matrimonial Agency*
(8)   March 31 *Mutt and Jeff in Turkey*
(9)   April 7   *Mutt's Moneymaking Scheme*
(10) April 14 *The Sultan's Harem*
(11) April 21 *Mutt and Jeff in Mexico*
(12) April 28 *The Sandstorm*
(13) May 5   *Mutt Puts One Over*
(14) May 12   *Mutt and Jeff*
(15) May 19   *Mutt and Jeff*
(16) May 26   *Pickaninni's G-String*
(17) June 2   *Mutt and Jeff*
(18) June 9   *Baseball*
(19) June 23   *The Californian Alien Land Law*
(20) June 30   *The Merry Milkmaid*
(21) July 7   *The Ball Game*
(22) July 24   *Mutt and Jeff*
(23) Aug. 4   *Mutt's Marriage*

(24)	Aug. 11	*Johnny Reb's Wooden Leg*
(25)	Aug. 18	*A Substitute for Peroxide*
(26)	Aug. 25	*Mutt and Jeff*
(27)	Sept. 1	*The Hypnotist*
(28)	Sept. 8	*The Mexican Problem*
(29)	Sept. 29	*Mutt and Jeff*
(30)	Oct. 13	*Mutt and Jeff*
(31)	Oct. 20	*Mutt and Jeff*
(32)	Oct. 27	*Mutt and Jeff*
(33)	Oct. 30	*Mutt and Jeff*
(34)	Nov. 13	*Mutt and Jeff*
(35)	Nov. 20	*Whadya Mean You're Contended*
(36)	Dec. 4	*Mutt and Jeff*

Mutt and Jeff Films Inc.
Producer: Harry "Bud" Fisher
Director/Animator: Charles Bowers
Distributor: Celebrated Players

1916

(37)	April 1	*Jeff's Toothache*
(38)	April 8	*Mutt and Jeff in the Submarine*
(39)	Aug. 12	*The Indestructible Hats*
(40)		*Cramps*
(41)		*The Promoters*
(42)		*Two for Five*
(43)		*The Dog Pound*
(44)		*The Hock Shop*
(45)		*Wall Street*
		(NB: 8 further films, titles not traced.)

Bud Fisher Film Corporation
Producer: Harry "Bud" Fisher
Directors: Charles Bowers, Raoul Barré
Animation: C.T. Anderson, Clarence Rigby, George Stallings, Ted
Sears, Mannie Davis, Burton Gillett, Dick Friel, Dick Huemer,
Ben Sharpsteen, Bill Tytla, Albert Hurter, Carl Lederer, F.M.
Follett, Isadore Klein
Distributor: Mutt and Jeff Film Exchange

1917

(46)	July 9	*The Submarine Chasers*
(47)		*The Cheese Tamers*
(48)		*Cows and Caws*
(49)		*The Janitors*
(50)		*A Chemical Calamity*
(51)		*The Prospectors*
(52)		*The Bell Hops*
(53)		*In the Theatrical Business*
(54)		*The Boarding House*
(55)		*The Chamber of Horrors*
(56)		*A Day in Camp*
(57)		*A Dog's Life*
(58)		*The Interpreters*
(59)		*Preparedness*
(60)		*Revenge Is Sweet*

Distributor: Fox Film Corporation

1918

(61)	March 24	*The Decoy*
(62)	March 31	*Back to the Balkans*
(63)	April 7	*The Leak*
(64)	April 14	*Freight Investigation*
(65)	April 21	*On Ice*
(66)	April 28	*Helping McAdoo*
		GB: *Coal and Cold Feet*
(67)	May 5	*A Fisherless Cartoon*
(68)	May 12	*Occultism*
(69)	May 19	*Superintendents*
(70)	May 26	*Tonsorial Artists*
(71)	June 2	*The Tale of a Pig*
(72)	June 9	*Hospital Orderlies*
(73)	June 16	*Life Savers*
(74)	June 23	*Meeting Theda Bara*
(75)	June 30	*The Seventy-five Mile Gun*
(76)	July 7	*The Burglar Alarm*
(77)	July 14	*The Extra Quick Lunch*
(78)	July 21	*Hunting the U-Boats*

(79) July 28   *Hotel de Mutt*
(80) Aug. 4   *Joining the Tanks*
(81) Aug. 11   *An Ace and a Joker*
(82) Aug. 18   *Landing a Spy*
(83) Aug. 25   *Efficiency*
(84) Sept. 1   *The Accident Attorney*
(85) Sept. 8   *At the Front*
(86) Sept. 15   *To the Rescue*
(87) Sept. 22   *The Kaiser's New Dentist*
(88) Sept. 29   *Bulling the Bolshevik*
(89) Oct. 6   *Our Four Days in Germany*
(90) Oct. 13   *The Side Show*
(91) Oct. 20   (title untraced)
(92) Oct. 27   (title untraced)
(93) Nov. 3   (title untraced)
(94) Nov. 10   *A Lot of Bull*
(95) Nov. 17   *The Doughboy*
(96) Nov. 24   *Around the World in Nine Minutes*
(97) Dec. 1   *Pot Luck in the Army*
(98) Dec. 8   *The New Champion*
(99) Dec. 15   *Hitting the High Spots*
(100) Dec. 22   *The Draft Board*
(101) Dec. 29   *Throwing the Bull*

1919
(102) Jan. 5   *The Lion Tamers*
(103) Jan. 12   *Here and There*
(104) Jan. 19   *The Hula Hula Cabaret*
(105) Jan. 26   *Dog-Gone Tough Luck*
(106) Feb. 2   *Landing an Heiress*
(107) Feb. 9   *The Bearded Lady*
(108) Feb. 16   *500 Miles on a Gallon of Gas*
(109) Feb. 23   *The Pousse Café*
(110) March 2   *Fireman Save My Child*
(111) March 9   *Wild Waves and Angry Women*
(112) March 16   *William Hohenzollern Sausage Maker*
(113) March 23   *Out an' In Again*
(114) March 30   *The Cow's Husband*
(115) April 6   *Mutt the Mutt Trainer*

(116)	April 13	*Subbing for Tom Mix*
(117)	April 20	*Pigtails and Peaches*
(118)	April 27	*Seeing Things*
(119)	May 4	*The Cave Man's Bride*
(120)	May 11	*Sir Sidney*
(121)	May 18	*Left at the Post*
(122)	May 25	*The Shell Game*
(123)	June 1	*Oh Teacher*
(124)	June 8	*Hands Up*
(125)	June 15	*Sweet Papa*
(126)	June 22	*Pets and Pearls*
(127)	June 29	*A Prize Fight*
(128)	July 6	*Look Pleasant Please*
(129)	July 13	*Downstairs and Up*
(130)	July 20	*A Tropical Eggs-pedition*
(131)	July 27	*West Is East*
(132)	Aug. 3	*The Jazz Instructors*
(133)	Aug. 10	*Oil's Well that Ends Well*
(134)	Aug. 17	*The Frozen North*
(135)	Aug. 24	*Sound Your "A"*
(136)	Aug. 31	*Hard Lions*
(137)	Sept. 7	*Mutt and Jeff in Switzerland*
(138)	Sept. 14	*All That Glitters Is Not Goldfish*
(139)	Sept. 21	*Everybody's Doing It*
(140)	Sept. 28	*Mutt and Jeff in Spain*
(141)	Oct. 5	*The Honest Book Agent*
(142)	Oct. 12	*New York Night Life*
(143)	Oct. 19	*Bound in Spaghetti*
(144)	Oct. 26	*In the Money*
(145)	Nov. 2	*The Window Cleaners*
(146)	Nov. 9	*Confessions of a Telephone Girl*
(147)	Nov. 16	*The Plumbers*
(148)	Nov. 23	*The Chambermaid's Revenge*
(149)	Nov. 30	*Why Mutt Left the Village*
(150)	Dec. 7	*Cutting Out His Nonsense*
(151)	Dec. 14	*For Bitter or for Verse*
(152)	Dec. 21	*He Ain't Done Right by Our Nell*
(153)	Dec. 28	*Another Man's Wife*

1920

(154)	Jan.	*A Glutton for Punishment*
(155)	Jan.	*His Musical Soup*
(156)	Jan.	*A Rose by Any Other Name*
(157)	Jan.	*Mutt and Jeff in Iceland*
(158)	Jan.	*Fisherman's Luck*
(159)	Jan.	*The Latest in Underwear*
(160)	Jan.	*On Strike*
(161)	Jan.	*Shaking the Shimmy*
(162)	Jan.	*The Rum Runners*
(163)	Jan.	*The Berth of a Nation*
(164)	Jan.	*Mutt and Jeff's Nooze Weekly*
(165)	Jan.	*Pretzel Farming*
(166)	Feb.	*I'm Ringing Your Party*
(167)	Feb.	*Fishing*
(168)	Feb.	*Dead Eye Jeff*
(169)	Feb.	*The Soul Violin*
(170)	Feb.	*The Mint Spy*
(171)	Feb.	*The Pawnbrokers*
(172)	Feb.	*The Chemists*
(173)	Feb.	*Putting on the Dog*
(174)	Feb.	*The Plumbers*
(175)	March	*The Great Pickle Robbery*
(176)	March	*The Price of a Good Sneeze*
(177)	March	*The Chewing Gum Industry*
(178)	March	*Hula Hula Town*
(179)	March	*The Beautiful Model*
(180)	March	*The Honest Jockey*
(181)	April	*The Bicycle Race*
(182)	April	*The Bowling Alley*
(183)	April	*Nothing but Girls*
(184)	April	*The Private Detectives*
(185)	April	*The Wrestlers*
(186)	April	*The Paper Hangers*
(187)	May	*The Toy Makers*
(188)	May	*The Tango Dancers*
(189)	May	*One Round Jeff*
(190)	May	*A Trip to Mars*
(191)	June	*Three Raisins and a Cake of Yeast*

S: Isadore Klein

(192)	June	*Departed Spirits*
(193)	June	*The Mystery of the Galvanised Iron Ash Can*
		aka: *The Great Mystery*
(194)	June	*The Breakfast Food Industry*
(195)	July	*The Bare Idea*
(196)	July	*The Merry Café*
(197)	Aug.	*In Wrong*
(198)	Aug.	*Hot Dogs*
(199)	Aug.	*The Politicians*
(200)	Aug.	*The Yacht Race*
(201)	Sept.	*The Cowpunchers*
(202)	Sept.	*Home Sweet Home*
(203)	Sept.	*Napoleon*
(204)	Sept.	*The Song Birds*
(205)	Oct.	*The Tailor Shop*
(206)	Oct.	*The Brave Toreador*
(207)	Oct.	*The High Cost of Living*
(208)	Oct.	*Flapjacks*
(209)	Oct.	*The League of Nations*
(210)	Oct.	*A Tightrope Romance*
(211)	Nov.	*Farm Efficiency*
(212)	Nov.	*The Medicine Man*
(213)	Nov.	*Home Brew*
(214)	Nov.	*Gum Shoe Work*
(215)	Nov.	*A Hard Luck Santa Claus*
(216)	Nov.	*All Stuck Up*
(217)	Dec.	*Sherlock Hawkshaw and Co.*
(218)	Dec.	*The North Woods*
(219)	Dec.	*On the Hop*
(220)	Dec.	*The Papoose*
(221)	Dec.	*The Hypnotist*
(222)	Dec.	*Cleopatra*
(223)	Dec.	*The Parlor Bolshevist*

1921

(224)	Feb. 26	*The Lion Hunters*
(225)	Feb. 27	*The Ventriloquist*

(226)	March 18	*Dr. Killjoy*
(227)	March 20	*Factory to Consumer*
(228)	April	*A Crazy Idea*
(229)	April 17	*The Naturalists*
(230)	May 7	*Mademoiselle Fifi*
(231)	May 7	*Gathering Coconuts*
(232)	May 7	*It's a Bear*
(233)	May 7	*The Far North*
(234)	May 14	*A Hard Shell Game*
(235)	May 7	*The Vacuum Cleaner*
(236)	May 21	*A Rare Bird*
(237)	May 21	*Flivvering*
(238)	June 11	*The Lion Hunters*
(239)	June 11	*The Glue Factory*
(240)	June 11	*Cold Tea*
(241)	June 12	*The Gusher*
(242)	June 26	*Watering the Elephants*
(243)	July	*A Crazy Idea*
(244)	July	*The Far East*
(245)	Aug.	*Training Woodpeckers*
(246)	Aug.	*A Shocking Idea*
(247)	Aug.	*Touring*
(248)	Sept. 17	*Darkest Africa*
(249)	Sept. 17	*Not Wedded but a Wife*
(250)	Sept. 17	*Crows and Scarecrows*
(251)	Sept. 17	*The Painter's Frolic*
(252)	Sept. 17	*The Stampede*
(253)	Sept. 17	*The Tong Sandwich*
(254)	Oct. 18	*Shadowed*
(255)	Oct. 18	*The Turkish Bath*
(256)	Nov. 26	*The Village Cutups*
(257)	Nov. 26	*A Messy Christmas*
(258)	Nov. 26	*Fast Freight*

1922

(259)	Jan.	*The Stolen Snooze*
(260)	Jan.	*Getting Ahead*
(261)	Jan.	*Bony Parts*
(262)	Jan.	*A Ghostly Wallop*

(263) Jan.   *Beside the Cider*
(264) Jan.   *Long Live the King*
(265) Jan.   *The Last Laugh*
(266) Feb.   *The Hole Cheese*
(267) Feb.   *The Phoney Focus*
(268) Feb.   *The Crystal Gazer*
(269) Feb.   *Stuck in the Mud*
(270) Feb. 27   *The Last Shot*
(271) March   *The Cashier*
(272) March   *Any Ice Today*
(273) March 12 *Too Much Soap*
(274) April   *Hoot Mon*
(275) April   *Golfing*
(276) April   *Tin Foiled*
(277) April   *Around the Pyramids*
(278) April   *Getting Even*
(279) May 15   *Hop, Skip and Jump*
(280) May   *Modern Fishing*
(281) May   *Hither and Thither*
(282) Aug.   *Court Plastered*
(283) Aug.   *Falls Ahead*
(284) Sept. 17 *Riding the Goat*
(285) Oct. 1   *The Fallen Archers*
(286) Oct. 8   *Cold Turkey*
(287) Nov. 12   *The Wishing Duck*
(288) Nov. 26   *Bumps and Things*
(289) Dec. 10   *Nearing the End*
(290) Dec. 23   *The Chewing Gum Industry*
(291) Dec. 30   *Gym Jams*

1923
(292) Feb. 4   *Down in Dixie*
                (further titles not traced)

Associated Animators
Director: Charles Bowers
Animation: Dick Friel, Burton Gillett, Ben Harrison, Manny
    Gould, Isadore Klein, Sid Marcus, George Rufle
Distributor: Short Film Syndicate

1925

(293)	Aug.	*Accidents Won't Happen*
(294)	Aug.	*Soda Clerks*
(295)	Sept.	*Invisible Revenge*
(296)	Sept.	*Where Am I?*
(297)	Oct.	*The Bear Facts*
(298)	Oct. 17	*Mixing in Mexico*
(299)	Nov. 14	*All at Sea*
(300)	Nov.	*Oceans of Trouble*
(301)	Dec. 5	*Thou Shalt Not Pass*
(302)	Dec. 12	*A Link Missing*

1926

(303)	Jan.	*Bombs and Bums* GB: *Bombs and Boobs*
(304)	Feb. 20	*On Thin Ice*
(305)	March 6	*When Hell Froze Over*
(306)	Apr.	*Westward Whoa*
(307)	Aug. 1	*Slick Sleuths*
(308)	Aug. 15	*Ups and Downs*
(309)	Sept. 1	*Playing with Fire*
(310)	Sept. 15	*Dog Gone*
(311)	Oct. 1	*The Big Swim*
(312)	Oct. 15	*Mummy o' Mine*
(313)	Nov. 1	*A Roman Scandal*
(314)	Nov. 15	*Alona of the South Seas*
(315)	Dec. 1	*The Globe Trotters*

9. Hy Mayer Cartoons

Universal/Imp Films
Producer: Carl Laemmle
Director/Story: Hy (Henry) Mayer
Animation: Hy Mayer, Otto Messmer

1913

(1)	March	*A Study in Crayon*

(2)	May 3	*Hy Mayer: His Magic Hand* (645)
		GB:*The Magic Hand*
(3)	May 31	*Hy Mayer: His Magic Hand* (545)
		GB: *Just for Luck*
(4)	June 7	*Pen Talks by Hy Mayer* (534)
		GB: *Pen Talk*
(5)	June 14	*Hy Mayer's Cartoons* (353)
(6)	June 21	*Filmograph Cartoons* (544)
(7)	June 28	*Fun in Film by Hy Mayer* (538)
		GB: *The Magnetic Maid*
(8)	July 5	*Sketches from Life by Hy Mayer* (444)
(9)	July 12	*Lightning Sketches by Hy Mayer* (444)
(10)	July 19	*In Cartoonland with Hy Mayer* (380)
(11)	July 26	*Summer Caricatures* (405)
(12)	Aug. 2	*Funny Fancies by Hy Mayer* (515)
(13)	Aug. 9	*The Adventures of Mr. Phiffles*
(14)	Aug. 16	*In Laughland with Hy Mayer* (400)
(15)	Aug. 23	*Pen Talks by Hy Mayer*
(16)	Aug. 30	*Hy Mayer: His Merry Pen* (460)
(17)	Sept. 6	*Humors of Summer* (480)
(18)	Sept. 13	*Hy Mayer Cartoons*
(19)	Sept. 20	*Antics in Ink by Hy Mayer*
(20)	Sept. 27	*Jolly Jottings by Hy Mayer* (980)
(21)	Oct. 4	*Whimsicalities by Hy Mayer* (500)
(22)	Oct. 11	*Hilarities by Hy Mayer* (500)
(23)	Oct. 18	*Leaves from Hy Mayer's Sketchbook*
		(308)

1914

(24)		*Pen Laughs* (500)
(25)		*Topical Topics* (465)
(26)	Sept.	*Topical War Cartoons* (500)
(27)	Oct.	*Topical War Cartoons No. 2* (500)
(28)	Nov.	*War Cartoons by Hy Mayer*

1923

| (29) | Dec. 8 | *A Movie Fantasy* |

10. *Bray Cartoons*

Bray Productions
Producer: John R. Bray
Animators: John R. Bray, Raoul Barré, L.M. Glackens
Distributor: Pathé-Eclectic

1913

(1) June 7   *The Artist's Dream*
                reissue: *The Dachshund and the Sausage*
(2) Sept. 6   *A Jungle Flirtation*
                GB: *A Lover's Trials*
                reissue: *Jocko the Lovesick Monk*
(3) Oct. 4   *A Wall Street Wail*
                GB: *The Strange Adventures of Smiling
                Sambo, Airman*
                reissue: *Exploring Ephraim's Exploit*

1914

(4) April 25   *The Grafters*
                GB: *A True Cat and Mouse Act*
                reissue: *When Mice Make Merry*
(5) Dec. 26   *Rastus' Rabid Rabbit Hunt*

1915

(6) Jan. 9   *Romiet and Julio*
                Animator: Raoul Barré
(7) May 29   *A Stone Age Adventure*
                Animator/Story: L.M. Glackens
(8) June 19   *When Knights Were Bold*
                Animator/Story: L.M. Glackens

11. *Old Doc Yak*

aka: *Doc Yak*
from the comic strip by Sidney Smith
Selig Polyscope Co.

Producer: William N. Selig
Director/Story/Animation: Sidney Smith

1913
  (1) July 11   *Old Doc Yak*
  (2) Oct. 29   *Old Doc Yak and the Artist's Dream*
  (3) Dec. 30   *Old Doc Yak's Christmas*

1914
   (4) Jan. 22   *Doc Yak Moving Picture Artist*
   (5) March 14   *Doc Yak Cartoonist*
   (6) April 11   *Doc Yak the Poultryman*
   (7) April 11   *Over the Fence and Out*
   (8) May 2   *Doc Yak's Temperance Lecture*
   (9) May 9   *Doc Yak the Marksman*
  (10) May 23   *Doc Yak Bowling*
  (11) May 30   *Doc Yak's Zoo*
  (12) June 6   *Doc Yak and the Limited Train*
  (13) June 11   *Doc Yak's Wishes*
  (14) Sept. 16   *Doc Yak's Bottle*
  (15) Oct. 15   *Doc Yak's Cats*
  (16) Oct. 24   *Doc Yak Plays Golf*
  (17) Dec. 8   *Doc Yak and Santa Claus*

Chicago Tribune Animated Weekly:
(inserts for newsreel)
Producer: Watterson Rothacker

1915
  (18) Sept. 18   No. 13: *Doc in the Ring*
  (19) Oct. 16   No. 18: *Doc the Ham Actor*

12. *Colonel Heeza Liar*

Bray Productions
Producer/Director/Story/Animation: John R. Bray
Distributor: Pathé

1913

  (1) Nov. 29 *Col. Heeza Liar in Africa*

1914

  (2) Jan. 10 *Col. Heeza Liar's African Hunt*
                   GB: *Col. Heeza Liar's Big Game Hunt*
  (3) March 14 *Col. Heeza Liar Shipwrecked*
  (4) April 18 *Col. Heeza Liar in Mexico*
  (5) May 18 *Col. Heeza Liar, Farmer*
  (6) Aug. 15 *Col. Heeza Liar, Explorer*
  (7) Sept. 26 *Col. Heeza Liar in the Wilderness*
  (8) Oct. 24 *Col. Heeza Liar, Naturalist*

1915

  (9) Feb. 6 *Col. Heeza Liar, Ghost Breaker*
  (10) Feb. 20 *Col. Heeza Liar in the Haunted Castle*
                   GB: *Col. Heeza Liar, Ghost Breaker: Second Night*
  (11) March 20 *Col. Heeza Liar Runs the Blockade*
                   In Pathé News No. 19
  (12) April 3 *Col. Heeza Liar and the Torpedo*
                   In Pathé News No. 21
  (13) April 10 *Col. Heeza Liar and the Zeppelin*
                   In Pathé News No. 23
  (14) May 8 *Col. Heeza Liar Signs the Pledge*
  (15) May 13 *Col. Heeza Liar in the Trenches*
                   In Pathé News No. 31
  (16) May 16 *Col. Heeza Liar at the Front*
                   In Pathé News No. 33
  (17) May 22 *Col. Heeza Liar, War Aviator*
                   In Pathé News No. 37
  (18) June 5 *Col. Heeza Liar Invents a New Kind of Shell*
                   In Pathé News No. 39
  (19) July 10 *Col. Heeza Liar, Dog Fancier*
  (20) July 31 *Col. Heeza Liar Foils the Enemy*
  (21) Aug. 21 *Col. Heeza Liar, War Dog*
  (22) Sept. 4 *Col. Heeza Liar at the Bat*
  (23) Dec. 28 *Col. Heeza Liar, Nature Faker*

1916

(24)	Jan. 6	*Col. Heeza Liar's Waterloo*
(25)	March 5	*Col. Heeza Liar and the Pirates*
(26)	April 27	*Col. Heeza Liar Wins the Pennant*
(27)	May 25	*Col. Heeza Liar Captures Villa*
(28)	June 22	*Col. Heeza Liar and the Bandits*
(29)	July 17	*Col. Heeza Liar's Courtship*
(30)	Aug. 17	*Col. Heeza Liar On Strike*
(31)	Aug. 24	*Col. Heeza Liar Plays Hamlet*
(32)	Sept. 14	*Col. Heeza Liar's Bachelor Quarters*
(33)	Oct. 11	*Col. Heeza Liar Gets Married*
(34)	Nov. 16	*Col. Heeza Liar, Hobo*
(35)	Dec. 21	*Col. Heeza Liar at the Vaudeville Show*

changed to ***Paramount-Bray Pictographs***

1917

(36)	Feb. 4	*Col Heeza Liar on the Jump*
(37)	Feb. 25	*Col. Heeza Liar, Detective*
(38)	March 19	*Col. Heeza Liar, Spy Dodger*
(39)	Aug. 20	*Col. Heeza Liar's Temperance Lecture*

Distributor: W.W. Hodkinson Corporation
Director/Story: Vernon Stallings

1922

(40)	Dec. 17	*Col. Heeza Liar's Treasure Island*

1923

(41)	Jan. 14	*Col. Heeza Liar and the Ghost*
(42)	Feb. 11	*Col Heeza Liar, Detective*
(43)	March 11	*Col. Heeza Liar's Burglar*
(44)	June 3	*Col. Heeza Liar in the African Jungles*
(45)	July 8	*Col. Heeza Liar in Uncle Tom's Cabin*
(46)	Aug. 5	*Col. Heeza Liar's Vacation*
(47)	Nov. 1	*Col. Heeza Liar's Forbidden Fruit* (730)
(48)	Dec. 1	*Col. Heeza Liar, Strikebreaker* (700)

1924

Distributor: Standard Cinema Corporation

(**49**) Jan. 1   *Col. Heeza Liar, Nature Faker* (650)
(**50**) Feb. 1   *Col. Heeza Liar's Mysterious Case* (820)
(**51**) March 1   *Col. Heeza Liar's Ancestors* (650)
(**52**) April 1   *Col. Heeza Liar's Knighthood* (700)
(**53**) May 1   *Col. Heeza Liar, Sky Pilot*
(**54**) June 1   *Col. Heeza Liar, Daredevil*
(**55**) July 1   *Col. Heeza Liar's Horseplay*
(**56**) Aug. 1   *Col. Heeza Liar, Cave Man*
(**57**) Sept. 1   *Col. Heeza Liar, Bull Thrower*
(**58**) Oct. 1   *Col. Heeza Liar the Lyin' Tamer*
(**59**) Nov. 1   *Col. Heeza Liar's Romance*

13. *Vincent Whitman Cartoons*

Lubin Manufacturing Co.
Producer: Sigmund Lubin
Director/Story/Animation: Vincent Whitman

1914

(**1**) March 14   *A Trip to the Moon*
(**2**) March 21   *The Bottom of the Sea*
(**3**) April 11   *A Strenuous Ride*
(**4**) April 25   *Another Tale*
(**5**) Oct. 3   *A Hunting Absurdity*
(**6**) Oct. 23   *An Interrupted Nap*
(**7**) Dec. 15   *The Troublesome Cat*

1915

(**8**) April 24   *Curses Jack Dalton*
(**9**) May 3   *A Hot Time in Punkville*
(**10**) May 21   *His Pipe Dreams*
(**11**) July 6   *Studies in Clay*
(**12**) July 12   *A Barnyard Mixup*
(**13**) July 15   *An African Hunt*
(**14**) July 26   *A One Reel Feature*
(**15**) Aug. 2   *Relentless Dalton*
(**16**) Aug. 16   *The Victorious Jockey*

14. *Hesanut*

Kalem Company

1914
- **(1)** Sept. 25 *Hesanut Hunts Wild Game*
- **(2)** Oct. 10 *Hesanut Buys an Auto*
- **(3)** Nov. *Hesanut Builds a Skyscraper*
- **(4)** Dec. *Hesanut at a Vaudeville Show*

1915
- **(5)** Jan. 16 *A Night in New Jersey*

15. *Joe Boko*

Producer/Director/Story/Animation: Wallace A. Carlson

1914
- **(1)** Oct. 10 *Joe Boko Breaking into the Big League*
  Distributor: Historic Feature Film Co.

1915
- **(2)** June 1 *Joe Boko in a Close Shave*
  Distributor: Essanay Film Mfg. Co.
- **(3)** Aug. 27 *Joe Boko in Saved by Gasoline*
  Distributor: Essanay Film Mfg. Co.

1916
- **(4)** April 4 *Joe Boko*
  in *Canimated Nooz Pictorial No. 8*
  Distributor: Essanay Film Mfg. Co.
- **(5)** Feb. 9 *Joe Boko's Adventures*
  Distributor: Powers-Universal

16. *The Police Dog*

Bray Productions
Producer: John R. Bray
Director/Story/Animation: C.T. Anderson
Distributor: Pathé

1914
  (1)   Nov. 21   *The Police Dog*

1915
  (2)   Feb. 20   *The Police Dog No. 2*
  (3)   March 27 *The Police Dog No. 3*
  (4)   May 1   *The Police Dog No. 4*
  (5)   June 12 *The Police Dog No. 5*
  (6)   July 24 *The Police Dog Gets Piffles in Bad*
  (7)   Sept. 25 *The Police Dog to the Rescue*

Distributor: Paramount

1916
  (8)   Jan. 27 *The Police Dog on the Wire*
  (9)   April 2 *The Police Dog Turns Nurse*
 (10)   May 7   *The Police Dog in the Park*
 (11)   June 6   *Working Out with the Police Dog*

Paramount-Bray Pictographs

1918
 (12)   March 4 *The Pinkerton Pup's Portrait*

17. Powers Cartoons

Producer: Patrick A. Powers
Distributor: Universal Pictures

1915
  (1)   Jan. 2   *Hunting in Crazyland* (517)
  (2)   Aug. 9   *To Frisco by the Cartoon Route*
                 Director/Story: Hy Mayer

1916
  (3)   Jan. 19 *Sammie Johnsin, Hunter*
                 Director/Story: Pat Sullivan
  (4)   Feb. 9   *Joe Boko's Adventures*
                 Director/Story: Wallace Carlson
  (5)   March 3 *Sammie Johnsin, Strong Man*
                 Director/Story: Pat Sullivan

(6) April 14 *Globe Trotting with Hy Mayer*
              Director/Story: Hy Mayer
(7) May 3   *Mr. Fuller Pep Tries Mesmerism*
              Director/Story: F.M. Follett
(8) May 17   *Mr. Fuller Pep Dabbles in the Pond*
              Director/Story: F.M. Follett
(9) May 31   *Mr. Fuller Pep Breaks for the Beach*
              Director/Story: F.M. Follett
(10) June 6   *Professor Wiseguy's Trip to the Moon*
              Director/Story: Joseph Cammer
(11) June 20 *Sammie Johnsin, Magician*
              Director/Story: Pat Sullivan
(12) June 22 *Such Is Life in China*
              Director/Story: Hy Mayer
(13) July 3   *Sammie Johnsin Gets a Job*
              Director/Story: Pat Sullivan
(14) July 20 *Jitney Jack and Gasolena*
              Director/Story: Jay Evans
(15) Aug. 10 *Sammie Johnsin in Mexico*
              Director/Story: Pat Sullivan
(16) Oct. 5   *Pen and Inklings Around Jerusalem*
              Director/Story: Hy Mayer
(17) Oct. 11 *Winsor McCay and His Jersey Skeeters*
              Director/Story: Winsor McCay
(18) Oct. 23 *Sammie Johnsin Minds the Baby*
              Director/Story: Pat Sullivan
(19) Nov. 8   *Motor Mat and His Fliv*
              Producer: Pat Sullivan
              Director/Animator: Otto Messmer
(20) Nov. 9   *High Life on a Farm*
              Director/Story: Hy Mayer
(21) Nov. 9   *A Pen Trip to Palestine*
              Director/Story: Hy Mayer
(22) Nov. 18 *Sammie Johnsin at the Seaside*
              Director/Story: Pat Sullivan
(23) Nov. 24 *Sammie Johnsin's Love Affair*
              Director/Story: Pat Sullivan
(24) Nov. 29 *The Trials of a Movie Cartoonist*
              Director/Story: Pat Sullivan

Animator: Otto Messmer
(25) Dec. 8 *Sammie Johnsin and His Wonderful Lamp*
Director/Story: Pat Sullivan
(26) Dec. 19 *Such Is Life in Alaska*
Director/Story: Hy Mayer
(27) Dec. 21 *Sammie Johnsin Slumbers Not*
Director/Story: Pat Sullivan
Animator: R. Eggeman

1917
(28) Jan. 3 *Boomer Bill's Awakening*
Producer: Pat Sullivan
Director: George Clardy
(29) Jan. 7 *The Trials of Willie Winks*
Producer: Pat Sullivan
(30) Jan. 14 *Mr. Fuller Pep Celebrates His Wedding
Anniversary*
Director/Story: F.M. Follett
(31) Jan. 20 *Fearless Freddie in the Woolly West*
Producer: Pat Sullivan
(32) Jan. 21 *Mr. Fuller Pep Goes to the Country*
Director/Story: F.M. Follett
(33) Feb. 4 *Mr. Fuller Pep's Wife Goes for a Rest*
Director/Story: F.M. Follett
(34) Feb. 14 *A Day in the Life of a Dog*
Producer: Pat Sullivan
Director: Will Anderson
(35) Feb. 18 *Mr. Fuller Pep Does Some Quick Moving*
Director/Story: F.M. Follett
(36) March 3 *The Tail of Thomas Kat*
Producer: Pat Sullivan
(37) March 4 *Mr. Fuller Pep: An Old Bird Pays Him a Visit*
Director/Story: F.M. Follett
(38) March 9 *The Love Affair of Ima Knut*
Producer: Pat Sullivan
Director: Otto Messmer
(39) March 11 *Mr. Fuller Pep's Day of Rest*
Director/Story: F.M. Follett
(40) March 21 *Inbad the Sailor*

Producer: Pat Sullivan

(41)   March 27 *The Ups and Down of Mr. Phool Phan*
       Director/Story: Milt Gross

(42)   March 31 *Boomer Bill Goes to Sea*
       Producer: Pat Sullivan

(43)   April 12 *A Good Story About a Bad Egg*
       Producer: Pat Sullivan

(44)   April 28 *A Barnyard Nightmare*
       Producer: Pat Sullivan

(45)   April 28 *Such Is Life in Algeria*
       Director/Story: Hy Mayer

(46)   May 14   *Cupid Gets Some New Dope*
       Producer: Pat Sullivan

(47)   May 14   *20,000 Laughs Under the Sea*
       Producer: Pat Sullivan

(48)   May 19   *When Noah's Ark Embarked*
       Director: John Colman Terry

(49)   May 26   *Them Were the Happy Days*
       GB: *Those Happy Days*
       Producer: Pat Sullivan
       Director: Otto Messmer

(50)   June 6   *A Pesky Pup*
       GB: *That Pesky Pup*
       Producer: Pat Sullivan
       Director: Joseph Harwitz

(51)   June 9   *Young Nick Carter Detectiff*
       Producer: Pat Sullivan
       Director: Will Anderson

(52)   June 18   *Duke Dolittle's Jungle Fizzle*
       Producer: Pat Sullivan
       Director: Charles Saxon

(53)   June 26   *China Awakened*
       Director/Story: Hy Mayer

(54)   July 3   *Monkey Love*
       Producer: Pat Sullivan
       Director/Animator: Ernest Smythe

(55)   July 7   *Seven Cutey Pups*
       Director/Story: Vincent Colby

(56)   July 10   *Box Car Bill Falls in Luck*

Producer: Pat Sullivan
Director/Animator: Bill Cause

(57) July 24   *A Good Liar*
Producer: Pat Sullivan
Director: Otto Messmer

(58) July 24   *A Barnyard Hamlet*
Producer: Pat Sullivan
Director/Animator: W.E. Stark

(59) July 24   *Hammon Egg's Reminiscences*
Producer: Pat Sullivan

(60) Aug. 6   *Seeing Ceylon*
Director/Story: Hy Mayer

(61) Aug. 10   *Colonel Pepper's Mobilized Farm*
Producer: Pat Sullivan

(62) Aug. 10   *Doing His Bit*
Producer: Pat Sullivan

(63) Oct. 15   *Seeing New York*
Director/Story: Hy Mayer

1918

(64) May 1   *New York by Heck*
Director/Story: Hy Mayer

18. *Bertlevyettes*

World Film Corporation
Producer/Story: Bert Levy
Director: Sidney Olcott
Live action and animation combined.

1915

(1) Jan. 4   *Great Americans Past and Present*
(2) Jan. 11   *Famous Men of Today*
(3) Jan. 18   *Famous Rulers of the World*
(4) Jan 25   *New York and Its People*

19. *M-in-A Cartoons*

M-in-A Films (Made in America Films)

Producer: David S. Horsley
Director/Story/Animation: Harry S. Palmer

1915

   (1)   Jan. 9   *The Siege of Liege*
   (2)   Feb. 6   *Great Americans*
   (3)   March 6 *The Dove of Peace*
   (4)   May 29   *Doctor Monko*

20. *Kriterion Komic Kartoons*

Pyramid Film Company
Producer/Director/Story/Animation: Harry S. Palmer

1915

   (1)   Feb. 12   No. 1   *(Taft Playing Golf)*
   (2)   Feb. 15   No. 2   *(Professor Dabbler)*
   (3)   Feb. 26   No. 3   *(Hotel de Gink)*
   (4)   March 5   No. 4   *(Industrial Investigation)*
   (5)   March 19 No. 5
   (6)   March 26 No. 6

21. *Pathé News*

Pathé Exchange
(Animated cartoons as a newsreel item.)
Bray Productions
Producer: John R. Bray
Directors/Animation: John R. Bray, W.C. Morris, Vincent Colby,
   J.D. Leventhal, L.M. Glackens, Flohri

1915

   (1)   Feb. 17   *The Boomerang*
   (2)   Feb. 24   *Our Defenses*
   (3)   March 3   *Hands Across the Sea*
   (4)   March 10 *The Presidential Chair*
   (5)   March 17 *Patriotism*
                     Director: Flohri
   (6)   March 20 *Col. Heeza Liar Runs the Blockade*
                     Director: J.R. Bray

(7) March 31 *A New Method of Fighting Submarines*
(8) April 3 *Col. Heeza Liar and the Torpedo*
Director: J.R. Bray
(9) April 7 *Some Feathers Fly in Turkey (Teasing the Eagle)*
(10) April 10 *Col. Heeza Liar and the Zeppelin*
Director: J.R. Bray
(11) April 14 *The Wily Jap*
Director: Flohri
(12) April 24 *The Resourceful Dachshund*
(13) May 8 *The Reward of Patience*
(14) May 13 *Col. Heeza Liar in the Trenches*
Director: J.R. Bray
(15) May 20 *Col. Heeza Liar at the Front*
Director: J.R. Bray
(16) May 23 *Col. Heeza Liar War Aviator*
Director: J.R. Bray
(17) May 28 *Another Fallen Idol*
Director: L.M. Glackens
(18) June 5 *Col. Heeza Liar Invents a New Kind of Shell*
Director: J.R. Bray
(19) June 26 *When Kitty Spilled the Ink*
(20) July 31 *The Dove of Peace*
Director: W.C. Morris
(21) Aug. 7 *Uncle Sam Gets Wise at Last*
(22) Aug. 14 *The Pilot of Peace*
Director: W.C. Morris
(23) Sept. 4 *Grandmothers of Yesterday, Today and
Tomorrow*
(24) Sept. 11 *Some Presidential Possibilities*
Director: W.C. Morris
(25) Oct. 2 *Dr. Worsen Plummer*
(26) Oct. 23 *Dumba's Departure*
(27) Oct. 30 *Dr. Worsen Plummer Starts a Drug Store*
(28) Nov. 6 *I Should Worry*
Director: Vincent Colby
(29) Nov. 13 *Wilson Surrenders*
Director: W.C. Morris
(30) Dec. 18 *Bubbling Bill*
(31) Dec. 22 *Troubles of a Pacifist*

1916

Directors/Animation: Charles Wilhelm, J.D. Leventhal, W.C. Morris, John C. Terry, A.D. Reed, Leighton Budd, L.M. Glackens

(32) March 8 *At It Again*
Director: Charles Wilhelm

(33) May 13 *Patience Is a Virtue*

(34) Sept. 2 *The Black List*
Director: W.C. Morris

(35) Sept. 20 *An Engineering Problem*
Director: J.D. Leventhal

(36) Sept. 23 *Responsibility for the War*
Director: W.C. Morris

(37) Sept. 30 *What Next*
Director: L.M. Glackens

(38) Oct. 7 *Misadventures of the Bull Moose*
Director: John C. Terry

(39) Oct. 14 *Hands Across the Sea*
Director: John C. Terry

(40) Oct. 21 *Are We Prepared for the International Trade Hunt*
Director: A.D. Reed

(41) Oct. 28 *The Courtship of Miss Vote*
Director: Leighton Budd

(42) Nov. 4 *The Pen Is Mightier Than the Sword*
Director: L.M. Glackens

(43) Nov. 11 *Somewhere in America*
Director: John C. Terry

(44) Nov. 25 *Now You See It Now You Don't*
Director: John C. Terry

(45) Dec. 2 *Our Merchant Marine*
Director: John C. Terry

(46) Dec. 9 *The Mexican Border*
Director: Leighton Budd

(47) Dec. 16 *Uncle Sam's Christmas*
Director: Leighton Budd

(48) Dec. 23 *Independent Poland*
Director: L.M. Glackens

(49) Dec. 30 *In Verdun Forests*

Director: Hugh M. Shields
continued as *Hearst-Pathé News*

22. Essanay Cartoons

Essanay Mfg. Co.

1915

(1)	March 3	*Introducing Charlie Chaplin*
		Director: Wallace Carlson
(2)	June 1	*Joe Boko in a Close Shave*
		Director: Wallace Carlson
(3)	Aug. 27	*Joe Boko in Saved by Gasoline*
		Director: Wallace Carlson
(4)	Dec. 22	*Mile a Minute Monty*
		Director: Leon Searl

23. The Animated Grouch Chaser

Thomas A. Edison, Inc.
Director/Story: Raoul Barré
Animation: Raoul Barré, Frank Moser
Combined live action and animation.

1915

(1)	March 4	*The Animated Grouch Chaser*
(2)	April 21	*Cartoons in the Kitchen*
(3)	May 22	*Cartoons in the Barber Shop*
(4)	June 5	*Cartoons in the Parlor*
(5)	June 21	*Cartoons in the Hotel*
(6)	July 8	*Cartoons in the Laundry*
(7)	Aug. 6	*Cartoons on Tour*
(8)	Aug. 25	*Cartoons on the Beach*
(9)	Sept. 9	*Cartoons in a Seminary*
(10)	Oct. 15	*Cartoons in the Country*
(11)	Oct. 29	*Cartoons on a Yacht*
(12)	Nov. 12	*Cartoons in a Sanitarium*
(13)	Dec. 4	*Black's Mysterious Box and Hicks in Night-mareland*

1916

(14) May 19   *The Adventures of Tom the Tamer and Kid Kelly*
(15) May 25   *The Story of Cook vs. Chef and Hicks in Nightmareland*
(16) June   *Love's Labors Lost*

24. Lederer Cartoons

Producer/Director/Story/Animation: Carl Francis Lederer
Distributor: Vitagraph

1915

(1) May 1   *Bunny in Bunnyland*
(2) May 27   *When They Were 21*
Distributor: Lubin Mfg. Co.

1915

(3) June 26 *Ping Pong Woo*
(4) Sept. 9 *Wandering Bill*

25. Dreamy Dud

Essanay Film Mfg. Co.
Producer/Director/Story/Animation: Wallace A. Carlson

1915

(1)   May 15   *A Visit to the Zoo*
(2)   May 15   *An Alley Romance*
(3)   June 1   *Lost in the Jungle*
(4)   June 7   *Dreamy Dud in the Swim*
(5)   June 22 *Dreamy Dud Resolves Not to Smoke*
(6)   June 30 *Dreamy Dud in King Koo Koo's Kingdom*
(7)   July 7   *He Goes Bear Hunting*
(8)   July 26 *A Visit to Uncle Dudley's Farm*
(9)   Aug. 9   *Dreamy Dud Sees Charlie Chaplin*
(10) Aug. 31 *Dreamy Dud Cowboy*
(11) Sept. 17 *Dreamy Dud at the Ole Swimmin' Hole*
(12) Oct. 14 *Dreamy Dud Up in the Air*
(13) Nov. 29 *Dreamy Dud in Love*

1916

(14) Jan. 22   *Dreamy Dud Lost at Sea*
(15) Sept. 27   *Dreamy Dud Has a Laugh on the Boss*
(16) Oct. 18   *Dreamy Dud in the African War Zone*
(17) Nov. 29   *Dreamy Dud Joyriding with Princess Zlim*

continued in **Canimated Nooz Pictorial**

1916

(18) Jan. 12   No. 4
(19) Feb. 22   No. 5
(20) March 3   No. 6
(21) March 23 No. 7
(22) June 7   No. 11
(23) July 5   No. 12
(24) July 26   No. 13
(25) Aug. 16   No. 14
(26) Sept. 6   No. 15
(27) Sept. 20   No. 16
(28) Oct. 11   No. 17

26.   Norbig Cartoons

Norbig Co.
Producer: Mr. Norton
Director/Animator: Joseph Cammer
Distributor: Powers/Universal

1915

(1) June 6   *Professor Wiseguy's Trip to the Moon* (500)

27.   Paul Terry Cartoons

Producer/Director/Story/Animator: Paul Terry
Distributor: Thanhouser Film Corp.

1915

(1) June 19   *Little Herman*
(2) Oct. 16   *Down on the Phoney Farm*

28. *Bobby Bumps*

Producer/Director/Story/Animator: Earl Hurd
Distributor: Universal "Joker"

1915

(1) July 3 *Bobby Bumps Gets Pa's Goat*
(2) Aug. 13 *Bobby Bumps' Adventures*

continued in **Bray Productions**
Distributor: Paramount

1916

(3) Feb. 24 *Bobby Bumps and His Pointer Pup*
(4) March 30 *Bobby Bumps Gets a Substitute*
(5) April 30 *Bobby Bumps and His Goatmobile*
(6) June 1 *Bobby Bumps Goes Fishing*
(7) June 29 *Bobby Bumps' Fly Swatter*
(8) July 24 *Bobby Bumps and the Detective Story*
(9) Aug. 11 *Bobby Bumps Loses His Pup*
(10) Sept. 7 *Bobby Bumps and the Stork*
(11) Sept. 28 *Bobby Bumps Starts a Lodge*
(12) Oct. 23 *Bobby Bumps Helps Out a Book Agent*
(13) Oct. 26 *Bobby Bumps Queers a Choir*
(14) Nov. 11 *Bobby Bumps at the Circus*

1917

(15) Feb. 11 *Bobby Bumps in the Great Divide*
(16) March 5 *Bobby Bumps Adopts a Turtle*
(17) March 26 *Bobby Bumps Office Boy*
(18) April 16 *Bobby Bumps Outwits the Dogcatcher*
(19) May 7 *Bobby Bumps Volunteers*
(20) May 28 *Bobby Bumps Daylight Camper*
(21) June 18 *Bobby Bumps Submarine Chaser*
(22) July 9 *Bobby Bumps' Fourth*
(23) Aug. 6 *Bobby Bumps' Amusement Park*
(24) Aug. 27 *Bobby Bumps Surf Rider*
(25) Sept. 17 *Bobby Bumps Starts for School*
(26) Oct. 8 *Bobby Bumps' World Serious*
       reissue: *Bobby Bumps Baseball Champion*

(27) Oct. 29 *Bobby Bumps Chef*
(28) Nov. 19 *Bobby Bumps and Fido's Birthday Party*
(29) Dec. 10 *Bobby Bumps Early Shopper*
          reissue: *Bobby Bumps Goes Shopping*
(30) Dec. 31 *Bobby Bumps' Tank*

1918
(31) Jan. 21 *Bobby Bumps' Disappearing Gun*
(32) Feb. 25 *Bobby Bumps at the Dentist*
(33) March 25 *Bobby Bumps' Fight*
(34) April 15 *Bobby Bumps on the Road*
(35) May 13 *Bobby Bumps Caught in the Jamb*
(36) June 10 *Bobby Bumps Out West*
(37) June 24 *Bobby Bumps Films a Fire*
(38) July 15 *Bobby Bumps Becomes an Ace*
          reissue: *Bobby Bumps Sharpshooter*
(39) Aug. 19 *Bobby Bumps on the Doughnut Trail*
(40) Sept. 30 *Bobby Bumps and the Speckled Death*
(41) Oct. 8 *Bobby Bumps' Incubator*
(42) Nov. 20 *Bobby Bumps in Before and After*
(43) Dec. 4 *Bobby Bumps Puts a Beanery on the Bum*

1919
(44) Jan. 24 *Bobby Bumps' Last Smoke*
(45) March 19 *Bobby Bumps' Lucky Day*
(46) April 16 *Bobby Bumps' Night Out with Some Night Owls*
(47) April 23 *Bobby Bumps' Pup Gets the Flea-enza*
(48) April 30 *Bobby Bumps Eel-ectric Launch*
(49) May 21 *Bobby Bumps and the Sand Lizard*
(50) June 25 *Bobby Bumps and the Hypnotic Eye*
(51) July 16 *Bobby Bumps Throwing the Bull*

continued in **Paramount Magazine**

1920
(52) April 4 *Bobby Bumps*
(53) April 25 *Bobby Bumps*
(54) May 16 *Bobby Bumps*
(55) June 6 *Bobby Bumps*

(56) July 11   *Bobby Bumps*
(57) Aug. 8   *Bobby Bumps the Cave Man*
(58) Sept. 19   *Bobby Bumps*
(59) Oct. 27   *Bobby Bumps*
(60) Nov. 14   *Bobby Bumps*
(61) Dec. 19   *Bobby Bumps' Orchestra*

1921
(62) Jan. 16   *Bobby Bumps*
(63) Feb. 20   *Bobby Bumps*
(64) March 13   *Bobby Bumps*
(65) March 20   *Bobby Bumps Checkmated*
(66) April 10   *Bobby Bumps*

continued in **Paramount Cartoons**

1921
(67) May 8   *Bobby Bumps Working on an Idea*
(68) July 9   *Bobby Bumps in Shadow Boxing*
(69) Aug. 21   *Bobby Bumps in Hunting and Fishing*

continued in **Bray Magazine**

1922
(70) Dec. 16   *Bobby Bumps at School*

continued in **Earl Hurd Comedies**

1922
(71) Dec. 2   *Railroading*

1923
(72) April 1   *The Movie Daredevil*
(73) June 2   *Their Love Growed Cold*

continued in **Pen and Ink Vaudeville**

1925
(74) Sept. 22   *Bobby Bumps and Co.*

29.   Earl Hurd Cartoons

Producer/Director/Story/Animation: Earl Hurd

1915
  (1) July 10   *Ski-Hi the Cartoon Chinaman* (245)
                    Distributor: Universal-Joker
  (2) Aug. 21 *The Troubles of Mr. Munk*
                    Distributor: Paramount

1916
  (3) April 15 *Teddy and the Angel Cake*
                    Distributor: Pathé Exchange

30.   Travelaughs

Powers
Producer: Pat Powers
Director/Story/Animation: Henry (Hy) Mayer
Distributor: Universal

1915
  (1) Aug. 9   *To 'Frisco by the Cartoon Route*

1916
  (2) April 14 *Globe Trotting with Hy Mayer*
  (3) June 22 *Such Is Life in China*
  (4) Oct. 5   *Pen and Inklings in and Around Jerusalem*
  (5) Nov. 9   *High Life on a Farm*
  (6) Nov. 9   *A Pen Trip to Palestine*
  (7) Dec. 19 *Such Is Life in Alaska*

1917
  (8) April 28 *Such Is Life in South Algeria*
  (9) June 26 *China Awakened*
 (10) Aug. 6   *Seeing Ceylon with Hy Mayer*
 (11) Oct. 15 *Seeing New York with Hy Mayer*

1918
 (12) May 1   *New York by Heck*
 (13) June 29 *Universal Screen Magazine No. 77*

(14) July 27   *Universal Screen Magazine No. 81*
(15) Aug. 3   *Universal Screen Magazine No. 82*
(16) Sept. 1   *Universal Screen Magazine No. 90*
(17) Oct. 12   *Universal Screen Magazine No. 92*
(18) Oct. 19   *Universal Screen Magazine No. 93*
(19) Oct. 26   *Universal Screen Magazine No. 94*

1919
(20) Jan. 18   *Universal Screen Magazine No. 105*

In *Pathé Review*
  Distributor: Pathé Exchange

1921
(21) Jan. 15   *Behind the Scenes of the Circus*
(22) March 5   *Water Stuff*
(23) March 26   *Spring Hats*
(24) April 30   *All the Merry Bow-Wows*
(25) May 29   *In the Silly Summertime*
(26) June 26   *The Door That Has No Lock*
(27) July 31   *A Ramble Through Provincetown*
(28) Sept. 4   *The Little City of Dreams*
(29) Sept. 18   *Day Dreams*
(30) Oct. 2   *Down to the Fair*
(31) Oct. 16   *Summer Scenes*
(32) Oct. 30   *All Aboard*
(33) Dec. 25   *Puppies*

1922
(34) Sept. 24   *How It Feels*
(35) Oct. 14   *In the Dear Old Summertime*
(36) Nov. 25   *Sporting Scenes*

1923
(37) Jan. 6   *Faces*

31. *Mile-a-Minute Monty*

Producer/Director/Story/Animation: Leon A. Searl
Distributor: Lubin Co.

1915

(1) Aug. 25 *Mile-a-Minute Monty*
(2) Sept. 14 *Monty the Missionary*

Distributor: Essanay
(3) Dec. 22 *Mile-a-Minute Monty*

32. Keeping Up with the Joneses

Gaumont Company
Producer/Director/Screenplay/Animation: Harry S. Palmer
Based on the comic strip by Arthur "Pop" Momand.

1915

(1) Sept. 13 *The Dancing Lesson*
(2) Sept. 22 (title unknown)
(3) Sept. 29 (title unknown)
(4) Oct. 6 *The Reelem Moving Picture Co.*
(5) Oct. 13 *The Family Adopt a Camel*
(6) Oct. 20 *Pa Feigns Sickness*
(7) Oct. 27 *The Family's Taste in Modern Furniture*
(8) Nov. 3 *Moving Day*
(9) Nov. 10 *The Family in Mexico*
(10) Nov. 17 *Pa Takes a Flier in Stocks*
(11) Nov. 24 *Pa Buys a Flivver*
(12) Dec. 1 *Pa Lectures on the War*
(13) Dec. 7 *The Skating Craze*
(14) Dec. 14 *Pa Sees Some New Styles*
(15) Dec. 21 *Ma Tries to Reduce*
(16) Dec. 28 *Pa Dreams He Wins the War*

1916

(17) Jan. 4 *The Pet Parrot*
(18) Jan. 11 *Ma Drives a Car*
(19) Jan. 23 *The Family Visits Florida*
(20) Jan. 30 *Pa Fishes in an Alligator Pond*
(21) Feb. 6 *Pa Tries to Write*
(22) Feb. 13 *Pa Dreams He Is Lost*
(23) Feb. 20 *Pa and Ma Have Their Fortunes Told*
(24) Feb. 27 *Pa Rides a Goat*

33. *The Canimated Nooz Pictorial*

Essanay Film Mfg. Co.
Producer/Director/Story/Animation: Wallace A. Carlson

1915

(1)	Oct. 1	No. 1
(2)	Nov. 10	No. 2
(3)	Dec. 13	No. 3

1916

(4)	Jan. 12	No. 4
(5)	Feb. 22	No. 5
(6)	March 3	No. 6
(7)	March 23	No. 7
(8)	April 4	No. 8
(9)	April 19	No. 9
(10)	May 24	No. 10
(11)	June 7	No. 11
(12)	July 5	No. 12
(13)	July 26	No. 13
(14)	Aug. 16	No. 14
(15)	Sept. 6	No. 15
(16)	Sept. 20	No. 16
(17)	Oct. 11	No. 17
(18)	Oct. 25	No. 18
(19)	Nov. 15	No. 19
(20)	Dec. 13	No. 20
(21)	Dec. 27	No. 21

1917

(22)	Jan. 10	No. 22
(23)	Jan. 24	No. 23
(24)	Feb. 10	No. 24
(25)	March 3	No. 25
(26)	March 17	No. 26
(27)	March 31	No. 27
(28)	April 28	No. 28

34. *Vernon Howe Bailey's Sketchbook*

Essanay Film Mfg. Co.
Producer/Director/Story: Vernon Howe Bailey

1915

   (1) Nov. 13   *Vernon Howe Bailey's Sketchbook*

1916

   (2) Jan. 29   ...*of Chicago*
   (3) March 1   ...*of London*
   (4) March 14 ...*of Philadelphia*
   (5) March 27 ...*of Paris*
   (6) April 14   ...*of Boston*
   (7) April 26   ...*of Rome*
   (8) May 20   ...*of San Francisco*
   (9) June 9   ...*of Berlin*
 (10) June 19   ...*of St. Louis*
 (11) July 10   ...*of New Orleans*
 (12) July 27   ...*of Petrograd*
 (13) Aug. 26 ...*of Washington*

35. *Phables*

International Film Service
Producer: William Randolph Hearst
Director: Gregory La Cava
Animation: Raoul Barré
Based on the comic strip by Thomas E. Powers.
In *Hearst-Vitagraph News Pictorial*

1915

   (1) Dec. 17   *The Phable of Sam and Bill*
   (2) Dec. 24   *The Phable of a Busted Romance*
   (3) Dec. 31   *Feet Is Feet: A Phable*

1916

   (4) Jan. 7   *A Newlywed Phable*
   (5) Jan. 14   *The Phable of a Phat Woman*
   (6) Jan. 21   *Cooks vs. Chefs: The Phable of Olaf and Louie*

36. *Hearst-Vitagraph News Pictorial*

International Film Service
Producer: William Randolph Hearst
Directors/Animation: Raoul Barré, Frank Moser, Leon A. Searl
Animated items for newsreel.

1915

(1) Dec. 17 *The Phable of Sam and Bill*
            Animator: Raoul Barré
            Story: Tom Powers
(2) Dec. 24 *The Phable of a Busted Romance*
            Animator: Raoul Barré
            Story: Tom Powers
(3) Dec. 31 *Feet Is Feet: A Phable*
Animator: Raoul Barré
Story: Tom Powers

1916

(4) Jan. 7 *A Newlywed Phable*
            Animator: Raoul Barré
            Story: Tom Powers
(5) Jan. 14 *The Phable of a Phat Woman*
            Animator: Raoul Barré
            Story: Tom Powers
(6) Jan. 18 *Who Said They Never Come Back*
            Story: Tom Powers
(7) Jan. 21 *Cooks Versus Chefs*
            Animator: Raoul Barré
            Story: Tom Powers
(8) Jan. 24 *Bang Go the Rifles*
            Story: Tom Powers
(9) Jan. 28 *Twas But a Dream*
            Animator: Raoul Barré
            Story: Tom Powers
(10) Jan. 31 *Mr. Nobody Home Buys a Jitney*
            Animator: Leon Searl
            Story: Tom Powers
(11) Feb. 4 *Poor Si Keeler*
            Story: Tom Powers

(12) Feb. 4 *Never Again, the Story of a Speeder Cop*
Animator: Raoul Barré
Story: Tom Powers

(13) Feb. 7 *Parcel Post Pete's Nightmare*
Animator: Frank Moser
Story: Tom Powers

(14) Feb. 11 *Old Doc Gloom*
Animator: Frank Moser
Story: Tom Powers

(15) Feb. 14 *Parcel Post Pete, Not All His Troubles Are Little Ones*
Director: Frank Moser
Story: Tom Powers

(16) Feb. 18 *Introducing Krazy Kat and Ignatz Mouse*
Animator: Frank Moser
Story: George Herriman

(17) Feb. 21 *Ignatz Believes in Dollar Signs*
Animator: Leon Searl
Story: George Herriman

(18) Feb. 25 *Krazy Kat and Ignatz Discuss the Letter "G"*
Animator: Frank Moser
Story: George Herriman

(19) Feb. 29 *Krazy Kat Goes a-Wooing*
Animator: Leon Searl
Story: George Herriman

(20) March 3 *Krazy Kat and Ignatz Mouse: A Duet*
Animator: Frank Moser
Story: George Herriman

(21) March 6 *Krazy Kat and Ignatz in Their One Act Tragedy*
Animator: Leon Searl
Story: George Herriman

(22) March 10 *The Joys Elope*
Animator: Raoul Barré
Story: Tom Powers

(23) March 13 *Krazy Kat Bugologist*
Animator: Frank Moser
Story: George Herriman

(24) March 17 *Krazy Kat and Ignatz at the Circus*

Animator: Leon Searl
Story: George Herriman
(25) March 20 *Krazy Kat Demi-tasse*
Animator: Frank Moser
Story: George Herriman
(26) March 24 *Krazy Kat to the Rescue*
Animator: Bill Nolan
Story: George Herriman
(27) March 27 *Krazy Kat Invalid*
Animator: Leon Searl
Story: George Herriman
(28) March 31 *Do You Know This Man*
Animator: Raoul Barré
Story: Tom Powers
(29) April 3 *Krazy Kat at the Switchboard*
Story: George Herriman
(30) April 7 *Krazy Kat the Hero*
Story: George Herriman
(31) April 14 *A Tale That Is Knot*
Animator: Bert Green
Story: George Herriman

37. *Kid Kelly*

Thomas A. Edison Co.
Animation: Frank Moser

1915

Series of cartoons included in *Animated Grouch Chaser.*

38. *Paramount-Bray Cartoons*

Bray Productions
Producer: John R. Bray
Distributor: Paramount

1916

(1) Jan. 6   *Col. Heeza Liar's Waterloo*
Director: John R. Bray
(2) Jan. 13   *Haddem Baad's Elopement*
Director: L.M. Glackens

(3) Jan. 20 *Inbad the Sailor*
            Director: C. Allen Gilbert
(4) Jan. 27 *The Police Dog on the Wire*
            Director: C.T. Anderson
(5) Feb. 3   *Farmer Al Falfa's Catastrophe*
            Director: Paul Terry
(6) Feb. 10 *Haunts for Rent*
            Director: C. Allen Gilbert
(7) Feb. 17 *Miss Nanny Goat Becomes an Aviator*
            Director: Clarence Rigby
(8) Feb. 24 *Bobby Bumps and His Pointer Pup*
            Director: Earl Hurd
(9) March 3 *How Dizzy Joe Got to Heaven*
            Director: L.M. Glackens
(10) March 5 *Colonel Heeza Liar and the Pirates*
            Director: John R. Bray
(11) March 12 *Farmer Al Falfa Invents a New Kite*
            Director: Paul Terry
(12) March 19 *The Chess Queen*
            Director: C. Allen Gilbert
(13) March 26 *Inbad the Sailor Gets into Deep Water*
            Director: C. Allen Gilbert
(14) April 2 *The Police Dog Turns Nurse*
            Director: C.T. Anderson
(15) April 9 *The Stone Age Roost Robber*
            Director: L.M. Glackens
(16) April 16 *Farmer Al Falfa's Scientific Dairy*
            Director: Paul Terry
(17) April 23 *Col. Heeza Liar Wins the Pennant*
            Director: John R. Bray
(18) April 30 *Bobby Bumps and His Goatmobile*
            Director: Earl Hurd
(19) May 6   *The Police Dog in the Park*
            Director: C.T. Anderson
(20) May 14 *Miss Nanny Goat on the Rampage*
            Director: Clarence Rigby
(21) May 20 *Col. Heeza Liar Captures Villa*
            Director: John R. Bray
(22) May 26 *Bobby Bumps Goes Fishing*

Director: Earl Hurd

(23) June 3   *Farmer Al Falfa's Tentless Circus*
           Director: Paul Terry
(24) June 10   *Kid Casey the Champion*
           Director: Frank Moser
(25) June 17   *Col. Heeza Liar and the Bandits*
           Director: John R. Bray
(26) June 26   *Bobby Bumps and the Fly Swatter*
           Director: Earl Hurd
(27) June 29   *Farmer Al Falfa's Watermelon Patch*
           Director: Paul Terry
(28) July 7   *The Wild and Woolly West*
           Director: A.D. Reed
(29) July 17   *Col. Heeza Liar's Courtship*
           Director: John R. Bray
(30) July 22   *Bobby Bumps' Detective Story*
           Director: Earl Hurd
(31) July 28   *In Lunyland*
           Director: Leighton Budd
(32) Aug. 4   *Farmer Al Falfa's Egg-citement*
           Director: Paul Terry
(33) Aug. 11   *Bobby Bumps Loses His Pup*
           Director: Earl Hurd
(34) Aug. 18   *Col. Heeza Liar Plays Hamlet*
           Director: John R. Bray
(35) Aug. 25   *Farmer Al Falfa's Revenge*
           Director: Paul Terry
(36) Sept. 1   *Bobby Bumps and the Stork*
           Director: Earl Hurd
(37) Sept. 9   *Col. Heeza Liar's Bachelor Quarters*
           Director: John R. Bray
(38) Sept. 16 *Farmer Al Falfa's Wolfhound*
           Director: Paul Terry
(39) Sept. 21 *Bobby Bumps Starts a Lodge*
           Director: Earl Hurd
(40) Sept. 27 *O.U. Rooster*
           Director: John R. Bray
(41) Oct. 9   *Farmer Al Falfa Sees New York*
           Director: Paul Terry

(42)	Oct. 17	*Col. Heeza Liar Gets Married*
		Director: John R. Bray
(43)	Oct. 23	*Bobby Bumps Queers the Choir*
		Director: Earl Hurd
(44)	Oct. 27	*Greenland's Icy Mountains*
		Director: L.M. Glackens
(45)	Nov. 3	*Farmer Al Falfa's Prune Plantation*
		Director: Paul Terry
(46)	Nov. 11	*Bobby Bumps at the Circus*
		Director: Earl Hurd
(47)	Nov. 17	*Col. Heeza Liar Hobo*
		Director: John R. Bray
(48)	Nov. 25	*What Happened to Willie*
		Director: L.M. Glackens
(49)	Dec. 1	*Farmer Al Falfa's Blind Pig*
		Director: Paul Terry
(50)	Dec. 11	*Bobby Bumps Helps Out a Book Agent*
		Director: Earl Hurd
(51)	Dec. 18	*Percy Brains He Has Nix*
		Director: H.C. Greening
(52)	Dec. 23	*Jack the Giant Killer*
		Director: L.M. Glackens

continued as **Paramount-Bray Pictographs**

39. *Sammie Johnsin*

aka: *Sammie Johnson; Sammy Johnson*
Pat Sullivan
Producer: Pat Sullivan
Animation: Pat Sullivan, R. Eggeman, Otto Messmer
Distributor: Powers-Universal

1916

(1)	Jan. 19	*Sammie Johnsin Hunter*
(2)	March 3	*Sammie Johnsin Strong Man*
(3)	June 20	*Sammie Johnsin Magician*
(4)	July 3	*Sammie Johnsin Gets a Job*
(5)	Aug. 10	*Sammie Johnsin in Mexico*

(6) Oct. 23 *Sammie Johnsin Minds the Baby*
(7) Nov. 18 *Sammie Johnsin at the Seaside*
(8) Nov. 24 *Sammie Johnsin's Love Affair*
(9) Dec. 8   *Sammie Johnsin and His Wonderful Lamp*
(10) Dec. 21 *Sammie Johnsin Slumbers Not*

40. *Silhouette Fantasies*

Bray-Gilbert Films
Producer: John R. Bray
Director/Story/Animation: C. Allen Gilbert
Titles/Verses: Oliver Hurford
Distributor: Paramount Pictures

1916

(1) Jan. 20   *Inbad the Sailor*
(2) Feb. 10   *Haunts for Rent*
(3) March 7   *The Chess Queen*
(4) March 15 *In the Shadows*
(5) April 8   *Inbad the Sailor Gets into Deep Water*
(6) May 10   *The Toyland Paper Chase*

41. *Joys and Glooms*

International Film Service
Producer: William Randolph Hearst
Director: Gregory La Cava
Animation: Frank Moser, Raoul Barré
Based on the newspaper cartoons by Thomas E. Powers.
In *Hearst-Vitagraph News Pictorial*

1916

(1) Jan. 24   *Bang Go the Rifles*
(2) Feb. 11   *Old Doc Gloom*
                Animator: Frank Moser
(3) March 10 *The Joys Elope*
                Animator: Raoul Barré

42. *Farmer Al Falfa*

Bray Productions
Producer: John R. Bray
Director/Story/Animation: Paul Terry
Distributor: Paramount

1916

(1) Feb. 3   *Farmer Al Falfa's Catastrophe*
(2) March 12   *Farmer Al Falfa Invents a New Kite*
(3) April 16   *Farmer Al Falfa's Scientific Dairy*
(4) June 8   *Farmer Al Falfa's Tentless Circus*
(5) July 9   *Farmer Al Falfa's Watermelon Patch*
(6) Aug. 10   *Farmer Al Falfa's Egg-citement*
(7) Aug. 19   *Farmer Al Falfa's Revenge*
(8) Sept. 18   *Farmer Al Falfa's Wolfhound*
(9) Oct. 18   *Farmer Al Falfa Sees New York*
(10) Nov. 3   *Farmer Al Falfa's Prune Plantation*
(11) Dec. 7   *Farmer Al Falfa's Blind Pig*

Distributor: Thomas A. Edison, Inc.

1917
(12) July 21   *Farmer Al Falfa and His Wayward Pup*

continued in *Paramount Magazine*
Distributor: Paramount

1920
(13) March 14   *The Bone of Contention*

continued in *Aesop's Fables*
Fables Pictures, Inc.
Distributor: Pathé

1923
(14) Feb. 23   *Farmer Al Falfa's Bride*
(15) Nov. 9   *Farmer Al Falfa's Pet Cat*

43. *Maud the Mule*

International Film Service

Producer: William Randolph Hearst
Director: Gregory La Cava
Animation: Bert Green
Based on the comic strip "And Her Name Was Maud" by Frederick
  Burr Opper.

1916
  (1) Feb. 4   *Poor Si Keeler*
  (2) June 5   *A Quiet Day in the Country*
  (3) July 3   *Maud the Educated Mule*
  (4) Oct. 2   *Round and Round Again*

44. Miss Nanny Goat

Bray Productions
Producer: John R. Bray
Director / Story / Animation: Clarence Rigby
Distributor: Paramount

Paramount-Bray Cartoons

1916
  (1) Feb. 17   *Miss Nanny Goat Becomes an Aviator*
  (2) May 14   *Miss Nanny Goat On the Rampage*

Paramount-Bray Pictographs

1917
  (3) April 6   *Miss Nanny Goat at the Circus*

45. Krazy Kat

International Film Service
Producer: William Randolph Hearst
Directors: Gregory La Cava, Vernon Stallings
Animation: Frank Moser, Leon A. Searl, Bill Nolan, Bert Green,
  Edward Grinham
Screenplays: H.E. Hancock
Based on the comic strip by George Herriman.

1916

In *The Hearst-Vitagraph News Pictorial*

- (1) Feb. 18   *Introducing Krazy Kat and Ignatz Mouse*
  Animator: Frank Moser
- (2) Feb. 21   *Krazy Kat and Ignatz Mouse Believe in Dollar Signs*
  Animator: Leon Searl
- (3) Feb. 25   *Krazy Kat and Ignatz Mouse Discuss the Letter "G"*
  Animator: Frank Moser
- (4) Feb. 29   *Krazy Kat Goes a-Wooing*
  Animator: Leon Searl
- (5) March 3   *Krazy Kat and Ignatz Mouse: A Duet, He Made Me Love Him*
  Animator: Frank Moser
- (6) March 6   *Krazy Kat and Ignatz Mouse in Their One Act Tragedy, The Tale of the Nude Tail*
  Animator: Leon Searl
- (7) March 13 *Krazy Kat, Bugologist*
  Animator: Frank Moser
- (8) March 17 *Krazy Kat and Ignatz Mouse at the Circus*
  Animator: Leon Searl
- (9) March 20 *Krazy Kat Demi-tasse*
  Animator: Frank Moser
- (10) March 24 *Krazy to the Rescue*
  Animator: Bill Nolan
- (11) March 27 *Krazy Kat Invalid*
  Animator: Leon Searl
- (12) April 3   *Krazy Kat at the Switchboard*
- (13) April 7   *Krazy Kat the Hero*
- (14) April 14 *A Tale That Is Knot*
  Animator: Bert Green

changed to *International Film Service Cartoons*

- (15) June 17 *Krazy Kat at Looney Park*
- (16) July 3   *A Tempest in a Paint Pot*
- (17) Oct. 9   *A Grid-iron Hero*
- (18) Nov. 27 *The Missing One*
  Animator: Leon Searl

(19) Dec. 19 *Krazy Kat Takes Little Katrina for an Airing*
Animator: Edward Grinham

1917
(20) Feb. 4 *Throwing the Bull*
(21) March 11 *Roses and Thorns*
(22) April 12 *Robbers and Thieves*
(23) April 29 *The Cook*
(24) May 27 *Moving Day*
(25) June 24 *All Is Not Gold That Glitters*
(26) Aug. 5 *A Krazy Katastrophe*

changed to *Bray Productions*
Producer: John R. Bray
In *The Goldwyn-Bray Pictographs*

1920
(27) Jan. 16 *The Great Cheese Robbery*
(28) Jan. 30 *Love's Labor Lost*
Director: Vernon Stallings
(29) March 3 *The Best Mouse Loses*
Director: Vernon Stallings
(30) April 14 *A Tax from the Rear*
Director: Vernon Stallings
(31) June 4 *Kats Is Kats*
Director: Vernon Stallings
(32) July 3 *The Chinese Honeymoon*
(33) Oct. 25 *A Family Affair*

1921
(34) Jan. 8 *The Hinges on the Bar Room Door*
Director: Vernon Stallings
(35) Jan. 26 *How I Became Krazy*
Director: Vernon Stallings
(36) Jan. 21 *The Awful Spook*
(37) Jan. 28 *Scrambled Eagles*
Director: Vernon Stallings
(38) Feb. 26 *The Wireless Wire-Walkers*
Director: Vernon Stallings

changed to **Winkler Pictures**
    Producer: George Winkler, Charles B. Mintz
    Production Manager: Nat L. Mintz
    Director: William C. Nolan
    Animators: Ben Harrison, Manny Gould
    Distributor: R.C. Pictures Corp.

1925

(39)	Oct. 1	*Hot Dogs*
(40)	Oct. 15	*The Smoke Eater*
(41)	Nov. 1	*A Uke-Calamity*
(42)	Nov. 1	*The Flight That Failed*
(43)	Nov. 15	*Bokays and Brickbats*
(44)	Nov. 15	*Hair Raiser*
(45)	Nov. 30	*The New Champ*
(46)	Dec. 1	*James and Gems*
(47)	Dec. 15	*Monkey Business*

1926
    Distributor: Film Booking Offices

(48)	Jan. 1	*Battling for Barleycorn*
(49)	Jan. 15	*A Picked Romance*
(50)	Feb. 1	*The Ghost Fakir*
(51)	Feb. 15	*Sucker Game*
(52)	March 1	*Back to Backing*
(53)	March 15	*Double Crossed*
(54)	April 1	*Scents and Nonsense*
(55)	April 15	*Feather Pushers*
(56)	May 1	*Cops Suey*
(57)	Sept. 2	*The Chicken Chaser*
(58)	Sept. 22	*East Is Best*
(59)	Oct. 11	*Shore Enough*
(60)	Oct. 25	*Watery Gravey*
(61)	Nov. 8	*Cheese It*
(62)	Nov. 22	*Dots and Dashes*
(63)	Dec. 6	*The Wrong Queue*
(64)	Dec. 10	*Gold Struck*

1927

(65)	Jan. 3	*Horse Play*

(66)	Jan. 17	*Busy Birds*
(67)	Jan. 31	*Sharps and Flats*
(68)	Feb. 14	*Kiss Crossed*
(69)	Feb. 28	*A Fool's Errand*
(70)	March 14	*Stomach Trouble*
(71)	March 28	*The Rug Fiend*
(72)	April 11	*Hire a Hall*
(73)	April 23	*Don Go On*
(74)	May 9	*Burnt Up*
(75)	May 23	*Night Owl*
(76)	June 6	*On the Trail*
(77)	June 20	*Passing the Hat*
(78)	July 4	*Best Wishes*
(79)	July 10	*Black and White*
(80)	July 18	*Wild Rivals*

Distributor: Paramount-Famous Lasky
Directors: Ben Harrison, Manny Gould

(81)	Aug. 1	*Sealing Whacks*
(82)	Aug. 13	*Tired Wheels*
(83)	Aug. 15	*Bee Cause*
(84)	Aug. 27	*Web Feet*
(85)	Aug. 29	*Skinny*
(86)	Sept. 10	*School Daze*
(87)	Sept. 24	*Rail Rode*
		aka: *Loco Motifs*
(88)	Oct. 8	*Aero Nuts*
(89)	Oct. 27	*Topsy Turvy*
(90)	Nov. 5	*Pie Curs*
(91)	Nov. 19	*For Crime's Sake*
(92)	Dec. 3	*Milk Made*
(93)	Dec. 17	*Stork Exchange*
(94)	Dec. 31	*Grid Ironed*

1928

(95)	Jan. 14	*Pig Styles*
(96)	Jan. 28	*Shadow Theory*
(97)	Feb. 11	*Ice Boxed*
(98)	Feb. 25	*A Hunger Stroke*

(99)   March 10 *Wired and Fired*
(100) March 24 *Love Sunk*
(101) April 7 *Tong Tied*
(102) April 21 *A Bum Steer*
(103) May 5 *Gold Bricks*
(104) May 19 *The Long Count*
(105) June 2 *The Patent Medicine Kid*
(106) June 12 *Stage Coached*
(107) June 30 *The Rain Dropper*
(108) July 14 *A Companionate Mirage*
(109) Aug. 4 *News Reeling*
(110) Aug. 16 *Baby Feud*
(111) Sept. 5 *Sea Sword*
(112) Sept. 15 *The Show Vote*
(113) Sept. 29 *The Phantom Trail*
(114) Oct. 15 *Come Easy, Go Slow*
(115) Oct. 29 *Beaches and Scream*
(116) Nov. 9 *Nicked Nags*
(117) Nov. 23 *Liar Bird*
(118) Dec. 7 *Still Waters*
(119) Dec. 22 *Night Howls*

1929
(120) Jan. 5 *Cow Belles*
(121) Jan. 18 *Hospitalities*
(122) Feb. 1 *Reduced Weights*
(123) Feb. 15 *Flying Yeast*
(124) March 1 *Vanishing Screams*
(125) March 15 *A Joint Affair*
(126) March 29 *Sheep Skinned*
(127) April 12 *The Lone Shark*
(128) May 10 *Golf Socks*
(129) May 24 *Petting Larceny*
(130) June 7 *Hat Aches*
(131) June 22 *A Fur Peace*
(132) July 6 *Auto Suggestion*
(133) July 19 *Sleepy Holler*
         (the last silent "Krazy Kat"; series continues
         with soundtrack)

46. *Paramount Pictographs*

Bray Productions
Producer: John R. Bray
Distributor: Paramount
(Magazine films with animated sequences.)

1916

(1)	Feb. 20	*Our Watch Dog*
		Director: J.R. Bray
(2)	Feb. 26	*The Bronco Buster*
		Director: J.R. Bray
(3)	March 12	*The Struggle*
		Director: J.R. Bray
(4)		and *In the Shadows*
		Director: C. Allen Gilbert
(5)	March 19	*The House in Which They Live*
		Director: J.R. Bray
(6)	March 26	*Watchful Waiting*
(7)		and *Found a Big Stick*
		Director: J.R. Bray
(8)	April 2	*Why?*
		Director: J.R. Bray
(9)	April 9	*The Long Arm of Law and Order*
		Director: J.R. Bray
(10)	April 30	*Miss Nomination*
		Director: J.R. Bray
(11)	May 14	*Fisherman's Luck*
		Director: J.R. Bray

47. *The Trick Kids*

Bray Studios
Producer: John R. Bray
Distributor: Paramount
In *Paramount Pictographs*
Animated dolls and toys.

1916

    (1)   Feb. 20   *The Birth of the Trick Kids*

(2) March 12   *The Strange Adventures of the Lamb's Tail*
(3) March 19   *Happifat's New Playmate*
(4) April 9   *The Magic Pail*
(5) April 23   *Happifat Does Some Spring Planting*
(6) April 30   *Happifat and Flossy Fisher's Unexpected Buggy Ride*
(7) May 7   *Happifat's Fishing Trip*
(8) May 21   *Happifat's Interrupted Meal*
(9) May 28   *Happifat Becomes an Artist and Draws a Bear*
(10) June   *Everybody's Uncle Sam*

48. *Plastiques*

Bray Studios
Producer: John R. Bray
Director/Animator: Ashley Miller
Distributor: Paramount
In *Paramount Pictographs*
Animated plaster models

1916
(1) Feb.   *Priscilla and the Pesky Fly*
(2) Feb.   *The Law of Gravitation*
(3) March   *Fifty-Fifty*
(4) April   *The High Cost of Living*
(5) May 7   *Did Sherman Say Law or War*
(6) July 9   *Why the Sphinx Laughed*

49. *Kartoon Komics*

Gaumont Company
Producer/Director/Story/Animation: Harry S. Palmer
Distributor: Mutual Pictures

1916
(1) March 4   *Our National Vaudeville*
(2) March 12   *The Trials of Thoughtless Thaddeus*
(3) March 19   (title unknown)

(4)	March 26	*Signs of Spring*
(5)	April 2	*Nosey Ned*
(6)	April 5	*The Greatest Show on Earth*
(7)	April 12	*Watchful Waiting*
(8)	April 19	(title unknown)
(9)	April 26	*Nosey Ned*
(10)	May 3	*Estelle and the Movie Hero*
(11)	May 10	*The Escapades of Estelle*
(12)	May 17	*As an Umpire Nosey Ned Is an Onion*
(13)	May 24	*Nosey Ned and His New Straw Lid*
(14)	May 31	*The Gnat Gets Estelle's Goat*
(15)	June 7	*The Escapades of Estelle*
(16)	June 14	*Johnny's Stepmother and the Cat*
(17)	June 21	(title unknown)
(18)	June 28	*Johnny's Romeo*
(19)	July 5	*Scrambled Events*
(20)	July 12	*Weary's Dog Dream*
(21)	July 19	(title unknown)
(22)	July 26	*Old Pfool Pfancy at the Beach*
(23)	Aug. 2	*Music as a Hair Restorer*
(24)	Aug. 9	(title unknown)
(25)	Aug. 16	*Kuring Korpulent Karrie*
(26)	Aug. 23	*Mr. Jocko from Jungletown*
(27)	Aug. 30	(title unknown)
(28)	Sept. 6	*The Tale of a Whale*
(29)	Sept. 13	*Nosey Ned Commandeers an Army Mule*
(30)	Sept. 20	*Pigs*
(31)	Sept. 27	*Golf*
(32)	Oct. 4	*Abraham and the Opossum*
(33)	Oct. 11	*Babbling Bess*
(34)	Oct. 18	*Inspiration*
(35)	Oct. 25	*I'm Insured*
(36)	Nov. 1	(title unknown)
(37)	Nov. 8	*Babbling Bess*
(38)	Nov. 15	*Haystack Horace*
(39)	Nov. 22	*What's Home Without a Dog*
(40)	Nov. 29	*Diary of a Murderer*
(41)	Dec. 6	*Our Forefathers*
(42)	Dec. 13	*Curfew Shall Not Ring*

(43) Dec. 20   *Twas Ever Thus*
(44) Dec. 27   *Mr. Bonehead Gets Wrecked*

1917
(45) Jan. 3   *Miss Catnip Goes to the Movies*
(46) Jan. 10   *The Gourmand*
(47) Jan. 17   *Mr. Common Peepul Investigates*
(48) Jan. 24   *Absent Minded Willie*
(49) Jan. 31   *Never Again*
(50) Feb. 7   *The Old Roué Visualizes*
(51) Feb. 14   *Taming Tony*
(52) Feb. 21   *Polly's Day at Home*
(53) Feb. 28   *The Elusive Idea*
(54) March 7   *Rastus Runs Amuck*
(55) July 14   *They Say Pigs Is Pigs*

50. Toyland

Taylor and Wheatley
Producers: R.F. Taylor, W.W. Wheatley
Director: Horace Taylor
Distributor: Powers
Animated dolls and toys.

1916
(1) March 9   *A Romance of Toyland*
(2) March 15   *A Toyland Mystery*
(3) April 12   *The Toyland Villain*
(4) May 10   *A Toyland Robbery*

51. Mr. Fuller Pep

Powers-Universal
Producer: Pat Powers
Director/Story/Animation: F.M. Follett

1916
(1) May 3   *He Tries Mesmerism*
(2) May 17   *He Dabbles in the Pond*
(3) May 31   *He Breaks for the Beach*

1917

- **(4)** Jan. 14   *He Celebrates His Wedding Anniversary*
- **(5)** Jan. 21   *He Goes to the Country*
- **(6)** Feb. 4   *His Wife Goes for a Rest*
- **(7)** Feb. 18   *He Does Some Quick Moving*
- **(8)** March 4   *An Old Bird Pays Him a Visit*
- **(9)** March 11   *His Day of Rest*

52.   Rube Goldberg Cartoons

Pathé Exchange
Story: Rube Goldberg
Animation: Raoul Barré, Bill Nolan, Gregory La Cava, George
Stallings

1916

- **(1)** May 8   *The Boob Weekly*
- **(2)** May 22   *Leap Year*
- **(3)** June 5   *The Fatal Pie*
- **(4)** June 19   *From Kitchen Mechanic to Movie Star*
- **(5)** July 3   *Nutty News*
- **(6)** July 17   *Home Sweet Home*
- **(7)** July 31   *Losing Weight*

53.   Charlie Cartoons

GB: *Star Cartoons*
Movca Film Service
Producer: S.J. Sangretti
Animation: John Colman Terry, G.A. Bronstrup, Hugh M.
Shields
Distributor: Herald Film Corp.

1916

- **(1)** May 15   *Charlie in Carmen*
- **(2)**   *Charlie's White Elephant*
- **(3)**   *Charlie Has Some Wonderful Adventures in
  India*
- **(4)**   *Charlie in Cuckoo Land*

(5)	*Charlie the Blacksmith*
(6)	*Charlie's Busted Romance*
(7)	*Charlie Across the Rio Grande*
(8)	*The Rooster's Nightmare*
(9)	*Charlie's Barnyard Pets*
(10)	*Charlie Throws the Bull*

54. Hearst-International News Pictorial

International Film Service
Producer: William Randolph Hearst
Animated items in newsreel.

1916

(1)	June 13	*Tom Powers Cartoon*
(2)	July 21	*On Again Off Again*
		Story: Tom Powers
(3)	Aug. 4	*Stripes and Patches*
		Story: Tom Powers

55. Hans and Fritz

Celebrated Film Corporation/Mutt and Jeff, Inc.
Producer: Harry "Bud" Fisher
Animation: Raoul Barré
Story: from the comic strip by Rudolph Dirks

1916

(1)	Aug. 12	*The Chinese Cook*

56. Keen Cartoons

Keen Cartoon Corporation
Producers: R.F. Taylor, W. Wheatley
Directors/Story/Animation: Charles F. Howell, Lee Connor,
    H.M. Freck

1916

(1)	Oct.	*Henry W. Zippy Buys a Motor Boat*
		Director: Charles E. Howell

(2) Oct.   *Slinky the Yegg*
              reissue: *Slick and Tricky*
              Director: Lee Connor
(3) Oct.   *Jerry McDub Collects Some Accident Insurance*
              reissue: *Zippy's Insurance*
              Director: H.M. Freck
(4) Dec.   *Henry W. Zippy Buys a Pet Pup*
              reissue: *Zippy Buys a Pet Pup*
              Director: Charles E. Howell
(5) Dec.   *Dr. Zippy Opens a Sanatorium*
              reissue: *Zippy in a Sanatorium*
              Director: Charles E. Howell

1917
(6) Jan. 1   *Mose Is Cured*
(7) Jan. 8   *The Old Forty-niner*
(8) Jan. 15   *Jeb Jenkins the Village Genius*
(9) Feb. 5   *Zoo-illogical Studies*
               reissue: *Dr. Bunny's Zoo*
(10) Feb. 12   *A Dangerous Girl*
               reissue: *She Was a Dangerous Girl*
(11) Feb. 28   *The Fighting Blood of Jerry McDub*
               Director: H.M. Freck
(12) March   *Mr. Coon*
(13) May 9   *When Does a Hen Lay*
               Director: Charles E. Howell

57. *Happy Hooligan*

International Film Service
Producer: William Randolph Hearst
Director: Gregory La Cava
Animation: Frank Moser, William C. Nolan, Ben Sharpsteen,
   Jack King
Screenplay: Louis De Lorme
Based on the comic strip by Frederick Burr Opper.

1916
(1) Oct. 9   *He Tries the Movies Again*

1917

(2)	Jan. 20	*Ananias Has Nothing on Hooligan*
(3)	March 25	*Happy Hooligan, Double Cross Nurse*
(4)	April 8	*The New Recruit*
(5)	April 26	*Three Strikes You're Out*
(6)	June 9	*Around the World in Half an Hour*
(7)	July 1	*The Great Offensive*
(8)	July 29	*The White Hope*
(9)	Sept. 2	*Happy Gets the Razoo*
(10)	Sept. 9	*Happy Hooligan in the Zoo*
(11)	Sept. 16	*The Tanks*
(12)	Oct. 7	*Happy Hooligan in Soft*
(13)	Oct. 16	*Happy Hooligan at the Picnic*
(14)	Oct. 16	*The Tale of a Fish*
(15)	Nov. 25	*The Tale of a Monkey*
(16)	Dec. 8	*Happy Hooligan at the Circus*
(17)	Dec. 16	*Bullets and Bull*

1918

| (18) | Jan. 13 | *Hearts and Horses* |
| (19) | Feb. 10 | *All for the Ladies* |

Distributor: Educational Pictures

(20)	April 19	*Doing His Bit* (450)
(21)	June 17	*Throwing the Bull* (465)
(22)	July 22	*Mopping Up a Million* (450)
(23)	Aug. 5	*His Dark Past* (450)
(24)	Aug. 12	*Tramp Tramp Tramp* (490)
(25)	Sept.	*A Bold Bad Man* (560)
(26)	Oct.	*The Latest in Underwear* (150)
(27)	Dec.	*Where Are the Papers* (500)

1919

(28)	Jan.	*Der Wash on Der Line* (600)
(29)	Feb.	*Knocking the "H" Out of Heinie* (800)
(30)	March 22	*A Smash-up in China* (500)
(31)	April	*That Reminds Me* (450)
(32)	June 22	*The Tale of a Shirt* (500)
(33)	June 29	*A Wee Bit o' Scotch*
(34)	July 20	*Transatlantic Flight*

(35) Aug. 24   *The Great Handicap*
(36) Sept. 7   *Jungle Jumble*
(37) Sept. 28 *After the Ball*
(38) Nov. 23   *Business Is Business*

continued in **Goldwyn-Bray Comic**

1920

(39) April 17 *The Great Umbrella Mystery*
(40) June 2   *Turn to the Right Leg*
(41) June 18   *All for the Love of a Girl*
(42) July 3   *His Country Cousin*
(43) Aug.   *Cupid's Advice*
(44) Sept. 11 *Happy Hooldini*
(45) Sept. 18 *Apollo*
(46) Oct. 25   *A Doity Deed*
                Director: William Nolan
(47) Oct. 27   *The Village Blacksmith*
                Director: Ben Sharpsteen
(48) Nov. 22   *A Romance of '76*
(49) Dec. 8   *Dr. Jekyll and Mr. Zip*
(50) Dec. 23   *Happy Hooligan in Oil*
                Director: William Nolan

1921

(51) Jan. 3   *Fatherly Love*
                Director: William Nolan
(52) Jan. 3   *Roll Your Own*
(53) April 29 *A Close Shave*

58. Walt MacDougall Cartoon

Associated Art Films
Producer: Louis J. Beck
Story/Designer: Walt MacDougall
Made for the Democratic Party.

1916

(1) Nov. 4   *Where Do You Go from Here*

59. *Jerry on the Job*

International Film Service
Producer: William Randolph Hearst
Directors: Gregory La Cava, Vernon Stallings
Screenplays: H.E. Hancock, Louis De Lorme
Animators: Will Powers, Walter Lantz
Based on the comic strip by Walter C. Hoban.

1916

(1)	Nov. 13	*Jerry Ships a Circus*
		Animator: Will Powers
(2)	Dec. 18	*On the Cannibal Isle*
		Animator: Will Powers

1917

(3)	Jan. 21	*A Tankless Job*
(4)	Feb. 18	*Jerry Saves the Navy*
(5)	May 20	*Quinine*
(6)	July 5	*Love and Lunch*
(7)	Aug. 19	*On the Border*

changed to **Goldwyn-Bray Pictographs**

1919

(8)	Sept. 6	*Where Has My Little Coal Bin*
		Director: Gregory La Cava
(9)	Nov. 10	*Pigs in Clover*
		Director: Gregory La Cava
(10)	Nov. 26	*How Could William Tell*
		Director: Gregory La Cava
(11)	Dec. 9	*Sauce for the Goose*
		Director: Vernon Stallings
(12)	Dec. 23	*Sufficiency*
		Director: Vernon Stallings

1920

(13)	Jan. 6	*The Chinese Question*
		Director: Vernon Stallings
(14)	Feb. 10	*A Warm Reception*

(15) Feb. 27 *The Wrong Track*
(16) March 9 *The Tale of a Wag*
(17) March 23 *A Very Busy Day*
　　　　 Director: Gregory La Cava
(18) April 21 *Spring Fever*
　　　　 Director: Gregory La Cava
(19) May 14 *Swinging His Vacation*
　　　　 Director: Gregory La Cava
(20) May 29 *The Mysterious Vamp*
　　　　 reissue: *Luring Eyes*
　　　　 Director: Gregory La Cava
(21) June 12 *A Punk Piper*
　　　　 Director: Vernon Stallings
(22) June 26 *A Quick Change*
　　　　 Director: Vernon Stallings
(23) July 16 *The Rhyme That Went Wrong*
　　　　 Director: Vernon Stallings
(24) July 27 *The Trained Horse*
　　　　 Director: Vernon Stallings
(25) Aug. 26 *Dots and Dashes*
　　　　 Director: Vernon Stallings
(26) Aug. 26 *The Train Robber*
　　　　 Director: Vernon Stallings
(27) Sept. 14 *Water Water Everywhere*
　　　　 Director: Vernon Stallings
(28) Oct. 2 *Jerry and the Five Fifteen Train*
　　　　 reissue: *The Return of the Five Fifteen*
　　　　 Director: Vernon Stallings
(29) Oct. 7 *Beaten by a Hare*
　　　　 Director: Vernon Stallings
(30) Oct. 7 *A Tough Pull*
　　　　 Director: Vernon Stallings
(31) Nov. 6 *The Bomb Idea*
　　　　 Director: Vernon Stallings
(32) Dec. 14 *A Thrilling Drill*
　　　　 Director: Vernon Stallings
(33) Dec. 28 *Without Coal*
　　　　 Director: Vernon Stallings

60. *Bringing Up Father*

International Film Service
Producer: William Randolph Hearst
Director: Gregory La Cava
Screenplay: Louis De Lorme
Animation: Frank Moser, Bert Green, Edward Grinham
Based on the comic strip by George McManus.

1916

(1) Nov. 21 *Father Gets into the Movies*
Animator: Frank Moser
(2) Dec. 14 *Just Like a Woman*
Animator: Bert Green

1917

(3) April 26 *The Great Hansom Cab Mystery*
(4) April 26 *A Hot Time in the Gym*
Animator: Edward Grinham
(5) June 7 *Music Hath Charms*
(6) Aug. 8 *He Tries His Hand at Hypnotism*

61. *The Katzenjammer Kids*

International Film Service
Producer: William Randolph Hearst
Director: Gregory La Cava
Screenplay: H.E. Hancock, Louis De Lorme
Animation: Gregory La Cava, John Foster, George Stallings
Based on the comic strip by Rudolph Dirks.

1916

(1) Dec. 11 *The Captain Goes A-Swimming*
Animator: Gregory La Cava

1917

(2) Jan. 8 *Der Great Bear Hunt*
Animator: George Stallings
(3) Jan. 26 *Der Captain Is Examined for Insurance*

Animator: Gregory La Cava

(4)	April 1	*Der Captain Goes A-Flivving*
(5)	April 12	*Robbers and Thieves*
(6)	April 26	*Sharks Is Sharks*
(7)	June 3	*20,000 Legs Under the Sea*
(8)	June 9	*Down Where the Limburger Blows*
(9)	July 8	*Der Captain Discovers the North Pole*
(10)	Aug. 25	*Der Captain's Valet*
(11)	Oct. 16	*By the Sad Sea Waves*
(12)	Oct. 16	*Der End of Der Limit*
(13)	Nov. 11	*The Mysterious Yarn*
(14)	Nov. 18	*Der Last Straw*
(15)	Dec. 2	*A Tempest in a Paint Pot*
(16)	Dec. 23	*Fat and Furious*
(17)	Dec. 30	*Peace and Quiet*

1918

(18)	Jan. 6	*Der Captain's Birthday*
(19)	Jan. 20	*Rub-a-Dud-Dud*
(20)	Jan. 27	*Rheumatics*
(21)	Feb. 10	*Policy and Pie*
(22)	Feb. 24	*Burglars*
(23)	March 3	*Too Many Cooks*
(24)	March 10	*Spirits*

Distributor: Educational Pictures

(25)	April 22	*Vanity and Vengeance*
(26)	May 6	*The Two Twins*
(27)	May 13	*His Last Will*
(28)	May 20	*Der Black Mitt*
		GB: *The Black Fist*
(29)	May 27	*Fisherman's Luck*
(30)	June 3	*Up in the Air*
(31)	June 10	*Swat the Fly*
(32)	June 24	*The Best Man Loses*
(33)	July 1	*Crabs Iss Crabs*
		GB: *Crabs Are Crabs*
(34)	July 8	*A Picnic for Two*
(35)	July 15	*A Heathen Benefit*

(36) July 19   *Pep*
(37) Aug.   *War Gardens*

continued as **The Shenanigan Kids**

62.   Dra-Ko Cartoons

Dra-Ko Film Company
Artist: Frank A. Nankivel

1916
Series of advertising films, titles untraced.

63.   Hearst-Pathé News

(Continuation of *Pathé News* and *Hearst International News Pictorial.*)
International Film Service
Producer: William Randolph Hearst
Directors: Gregory La Cava, F.M. Follett, Leighton Budd, Hal Coffman
Animated items in newsreels.

1917
  (1) Jan. 3   *Help Wanted*
                 Director: F.M. Follett
  (2) Jan. 10   *A Hard Cold Winter*
  (3) Jan. 13   *Oh Girls What Next*
                 Director: Leighton Budd
  (4) Jan. 20   *The Mexican Crisis*
                 Director: F.M. Follett
  (5) Jan. 27   *Billy Sunday's Tabernacle*
                 Director: F.M. Follett
  (6) Feb. 14   *Up a Stump*
  (7) March 10 *Freedom of the Seas*
  (8) March 21 *Adventures of Mr. Common People*
  (9) March 24 *Solid Comfort*
(10) March 28 *Mr. Common People's Busy Day*

(11) March 31 *Peace Insurance*
(12) April 11 *Cartoon*
(13) April 21 *Heroes of the Past*
(14) April 28 *The Great Offensive*
(15) May 2 *Mr. Slacker*
(16) May 5 *Potato Is King*
(17) May 16 *Her Crowning Achievement*
(18) May 23 *Have You Bought Your Liberty Bond*
(19) May 26 *Both Good Soldiers*
(20) May 30 *When Will He Throw Off This Burden*
(21) June 2 *In the Garden Trenches*
(22) June 9 *Ten Million Men from Uncle Sam*
(23) June 13 *Liberty Loan of 1917*
(24) July 4 *A Regular Man*
(25) July 14 *The Awakening*
Director: Hal Coffman
(26) July 18 *America Does Not Forget*
(27) Aug. 4 *They All Look Alike to Me*
(28) Aug. 15 *Growing Fast*
(29) Sept. 5 *Hoch the Kaiser*
(30) Sept. 12 *Fall Styles for Men*
(31) Oct. 13 *Buy a Liberty Bond*
(32) Nov. 4 *It Has Come at Last*
(33) Nov. 28 *Which?*
(34) Dec. 1 *The Handwriting in the Sky*

1918
(35) Jan. 19 *Dropping the Mask*
(36) Jan. 30 *Every Little Bit Helps*
(37) Feb. 9 *A New Shadow Haunts Autocracy*
(38) Feb. 12 *Progress*
(39) Feb. 15 *The Heritage*
(40) Feb. 20 *The Threatening Storm*
(41) Feb. 23 *The Glutton*
(42) March 2 *Cartoon*
(43) March 13 *Making an Example of Him*
(44) April 6 *Join the Land Army*
(45) April 13 *Cartoon*
(46) April 20 *Give Him a Helping Hand*

64. *Paramount-Bray Pictographs*

Bray Productions
Producer: John R. Bray
Distributor: Paramount
Magazine films with animated sequences.

1917

(1) Feb. 4   *Col. Heeza Liar on the Jump*
                Director: John R. Bray

(2) Feb. 11 *Bobby Bumps in the Great Divide*
                Director: Earl Hurd

(3) Feb. 18 *Quacky Doodles' Picnic*
                Director: F.M. Follett

(4) Feb. 25 *Col. Heeza Liar Detective*
                Director: John R. Bray

(5) March 5 *Bobby Bumps Adopts a Turtle*
                Director: Earl Hurd

(6) March 12 *Quacky Doodles' Food Crisis*
                Director: F.M. Follett

(7) March 19 *Col. Heeza Liar Spy Dodger*
                Director: John R. Bray

(8) and   *Picto Puzzles* by Sam Loyd

(9) March 26 *Bobby Bumps Office Boy*
                Director: Earl Hurd

(10) April 2 *Quacky Doodles as the Early Bird*
                Director: F.M. Follett

(11) and   *Picto Puzzles* by Sam Loyd

(12) April 9 *Miss Nanny Goat at the Circus*
                Director: Clarence Rigby

(13) April 16 *Bobby Bumps Outwits the Dog Catcher*
                Director: Earl Hurd

(14) and   *Picto Puzzles* by Sam Loyd

(15) April 23 *Quacky Doodles Soldiering for Fair*
                Director: F.M. Follett

(16) April 30 *Stung*
                Director: Leighton Budd

(17) May 7 *Bobby Bumps Volunteers*
                Director: Earl Hurd

(18) May 14 *The Submarine Mine-Layer*

		Director: J.D. Leventhal
(19)	and	*Picto Puzzles* by Sam Loyd
(20)	May 21	*The Awakening of America*
(21)	and	*Picto Puzzles* by Sam Loyd
(22)	May 28	*Bobby Bumps Daylight Camper*
		Director: Earl Hurd
(23)	June 4	*Otto Luck in the Movies*
		Director: Wallace Carlson
(24)	June 11	*Traveling Forts*
		Director: J.D. Leventhal
(25)	and	*Evolution of the Dachshund*
		Director: Leighton Budd
(26)	June 18	*Bobby Bumps Submarine Chaser*
		Director: Earl Hurd
(27)	June 25	*Otto Luck to the Rescue*
		Director: Wallace Carlson
(28)	July 2	*Mechanical Operation of British Tanks*
		Director: J.D. Leventhal
(29)	and	*Picto Puzzles* by Sam Loyd
(30)	July 9	*Bobby Bumps' Fourth*
		Director: Earl Hurd
(31)	July 16	*Otto Luck and Ruby Razmataz*
		Director: Wallace Carlson
(32)	July 23	*Sic 'Em Cat*
		Director: Leighton Budd
(33)	July 30	*Fiske Torpedo Plane*
		Director: J.D. Leventhal
(34)	and	*Picto Puzzles* by Sam Loyd
(35)	Aug. 6	*Bobby Bumps' Amusement Park*
		Director: Earl Hurd
(36)	Aug. 13	*Otto Luck's Flivvered Romance*
		Director: Wallace Carlson
(37)	Aug. 20	*Uncle Sam's Dinner Party*
		Director: Leighton Budd
(38)	Aug. 27	*Bobby Bumps Surf Rider*
		Director: Earl Hurd
(39)	Sept. 3	*Goodrich Dirt Among the Beach Nuts*
		Director: Wallace Carlson
(40)	Sept. 10	*Quacky Doodles Signs the Pledge*

Director: F.M. Follett
(41) Sept. 17 *Bobby Bumps Starts for School*
Director: Earl Hurd
(42) Sept. 24 *A Submarine Destroyer*
Director: J.D. Leventhal
(43) Oct. 1 *Goodrich Dirt Lunch Detective*
Director: Wallace Carlson
(44) Oct. 8 *Bobby Bumps' World Serious*
Director: Earl Hurd
(45) Oct. 15 *Quacky Doodles the Cheater*
Director: F.M. Follett
(46) Oct. 22 *The Aeroplane Machine Gun*
Director: J.D. Leventhal
(47) Oct. 29 *Bobby Bumps, Chef*
Director: Earl Hurd
(48) Nov. 5 *Goodrich Dirt at the Training Camp*
Director: Wallace Carlson
(49) Nov. 12 *Putting Volcanoes to Work*
Director: J.D. Leventhal
(50) Nov. 19 *Bobby Bumps and Fido's Birthday Party*
Director: Earl Hurd
(51) Nov. 26 *The Gasoline Engine*
Director: J.D. Leventhal
(52) Dec. 3 *Goodrich Dirt at the Amateur Show*
Director: Wallace Carlson
(53) Dec. 10 *Bobby Bumps Early Shopper*
Director: Earl Hurd
(54) Dec. 17 *Freak Patents: The Balloon R.R.*
Director: J.D. Leventhal
(55) Dec. 24 *Goodrich Dirt and the $1000 Reward*
Director: Wallace Carlson

1918
(56) Jan. 7 *Goodrich Dirt and the Duke de Whatanob*
Director: Wallace Carlson
(57) Jan. 14 *The Panama Canal*
Director: J.D. Leventhal
(58) Jan. 21 *Bobby Bumps' Disappearing Gun*
Director: Earl Hurd

(59) Jan. 28   *The Peril of Prussianism*
Director: Leighton Budd

(60) Feb. 4   *Putting Fritz on the Water Wagon*
Director: Leighton Budd

(61) Feb. 11   *Goodrich Dirt's Bear Facts*
Director: Wallace Carlson

(62) Feb. 18   *The Rudiments of Flying*
Director: J.D. Leventhal

(63) Feb. 25   *Bobby Bumps at the Dentist*
Director: Earl Hurd

(64) March 4   *The Pinkerton Pup's Portrait*
Director: C.T. Anderson

(65) March 11   *The Torpedo, Hornet of the Sea*
Director: J.D. Leventhal

(66) March 18   *Goodrich Dirt in the Barber Business*
Director: Wallace Carlson

(67) March 25   *Bobby Bumps' Fight*
Director: Earl Hurd

(68) April 1   *Me Und Gott*
Director: L.M. Glackens

(69) April 8   *Goodrich Dirt Mat Artist*
Director: Wallace Carlson

(70) April 15   *Bobby Bumps on the Road*
Director: Earl Hurd

(71) April 22   *A Tonsorial Slot Machine*
Director: Leighton Budd

(72) April 29   *The Third Liberty Loan Bomb*
Director: Leighton Budd

(73) May 6   *Goodrich Dirt Bad Man Tamer*
Director: Wallace Carlson

(74) May 13   *Bobby Bumps Caught in the Jamb*
Director: Earl Hurd

(75) May 20   *The Depth Bomb*
Director: E. Dean Parmelee

(76) May 27   *Goodrich Dirt in Darkest Africa*
Director: Wallace Carlson

(77) June 3   *Bobby Bumps Out West*
Director: Earl Hurd

(78) June 10   *Out of the Inkwell*

Director: Max Fleischer
(79) June 17 *Goodrich Dirt King of Spades*
Director: Wallace Carlson
(80) June 24 *Bobby Bumps Films a Fire*
Director: Earl Hurd
(81) July 1 *The First Flyer*
Director: L.M. Glackens
(82) and *Animated Technical Drawings*
Director: E. Dean Parmelee
(83) July 8 *Goodrich Dirt the Cop*
Director: Wallace Carlson
(84) July 15 *Bobby Bumps Becomes an Ace*
Director: Earl Hurd
(85) July 22 *Von Loon's 25,000 Mile Gun*
Director: L.M. Glackens
(86) July 29 *Animated Technical Drawing*
Director: E. Dean Parmelee
(87) Aug. 5 *Goodrich Dirt the Dark and Stormy Knight*
Director: Wallace Carlson
(88) Aug. 12 *The Kaiser's Surprise Party*
Director: Leighton Budd
(89) Aug. 19 *Bobby Bumps on the Doughnut Trail*
Director: Earl Hurd
(90) Aug. 26 *Goodrich Dirt Coin Collector*
Director: Wallace Carlson
(91) Sept. 2 *Aerial Warfare*
Director: E. Dean Parmelee
(92) Sept. 9 *A Watched Pot*
Director: Santry
(93) Sept. 16 *Cartoon* (title untraced)
(94) Sept. 23 *Bobby Bumps and the Speckled Death*
Director: Earl Hurd
(95) Sept. 30 *Goodrich Dirt Millionaire*
Director: Wallace Carlson
(96) Oct. 1 *Von Loon's Non-Capturable Aeroplane*
Director: L.M. Glackens
(97) Oct. 8 *Bobby Bumps' Incubator*
Director: Earl Hurd
(98) Oct. 15 *Cartoon* (title untraced)

(99)	Oct. 22	*The Greased Pole*
		Director: Leighton Budd
(100)	Oct. 29	*Goodrich Dirt When Wishes Come True*
		Director: Wallace Carlson
(101)	Nov. 6	*A German Trick That Failed*
		Director: Leighton Budd
(102)	Nov. 13	*Cartoon* (title untraced)
(103)	Nov. 20	*Bobby Bumps in Before and After*
		Director: Earl Hurd
(104)	Nov. 27	*Uncle Sam's Coming Problem*
		Director: Leighton Budd
(105)	Dec. 4	*Bobby Bumps Puts a Beanery on the Bum*
		Director: Earl Hurd
(106)	Dec. 11	*Goodrich Dirt Cowpuncher*
		Director: Wallace Carlson
(107)	Dec. 18	*Pictures in the Fire*
		aka: *Faces in the Fire*
		Director: Santry
(108)	Dec. 25	*Goodrich Dirt in Spot Goes Romeoing*
		Director: Wallace Carlson

1919

(109)	Jan. 1	*Cartoon* (title untraced)
(110)	Jan. 8	*Bobby Bumps' Last Smoke*
		Director: Earl Hurd
(111)	Jan. 15	*Private Bass His Pass*
		Director: L.M. Glackens
(112)	Jan. 22	*Goodrich Dirt in a Difficult Delivery*
		Director: Wallace Carlson
(113)	Jan. 29	*The Adventures of Hardrock Dome*
		Director: Pat Sullivan
(114)	Feb. 5	*The Adventures of Hardrock Dome No. 2*
		Director: Pat Sullivan
(115)	Feb. 12	*The Further Adventures of Hardrock Dome*
		Director: Pat Sullivan
(116)	Feb. 19	*Theory of the Long Range Shell*
		Director: E. Dean Parmelee
(117)	Feb. 26	*Goodrich Dirt Hypnotist*
		Director: Wallace Carlson

(118) March 5   *Out of the Inkwell*
                      Director: Max Fleischer
(119) March 12 *Theory of the Hand Grenade*
                      Director: E. Dean Parmelee
(120) March 19 *Bobby Bumps' Lucky Day*
                      Director: Earl Hurd
(121) March 26 *Dud Perkins Gets Mortified*
                      Director: Wallace Carlson
(122) April 2   *Out of the Inkwell*
                      Director: Max Fleischer
(123) April 9   *The Parson*
                      Director: Wallace Carlson
(124) April 16 *Bobby Bumps' Night Out with Some Night Owls*
                      Director: Earl Hurd
(125) April 23 *Bobby Bumps' Pup Gets the Flea-enza*
                      Director: Earl Hurd
(126) April 30 *Bobby Bumps' Eel-lectric Launch*
                      Director: Earl Hurd
(127) May 7   *Wounded by the Beauty*
                      Director: Wallace Carlson
(128) May 14 *Dud the Circus Performer*
                      Director: Wallace Carlson
(129) May 21 *Bobby Bumps and the Sand Lizard*
                      Director: Earl Hurd
(130) May 28 *In 1998 A.D.: The Automatic Reducing Machine*
                      Director: Leighton Budd
(131) June 4   *Dud's Greatest Cirkus on Earth*
                      Director: Wallace Carlson
(132) June 11 *The Biography of Madame Fashion*
                      Director: L.M. Glackens
(133) June 18 *Cartoon* (title untraced)
(134) June 25 *Bobby Bumps and the Hypnotic Eye*
                      Director: Earl Hurd
(135) July 2   *Cartoon* (title untraced)
(136) July 9   *At the Ol' Swimmin' Hole*
                      Director: Wallace Carlson
(137) July 16 *Bobby Bumps Throwing the Bull*

Director: Earl Hurd
(138) July 23   *Cartoon* (title untraced)
(139) July 30   *Tying the Nuptial Knot*
Director: L.M. Glackens

continued as *Goldwyn-Bray Pictograph*

65.   Quacky Doodles

Bray Productions
Producer: John R. Bray
Animation: F.M. Follett
Based on the comic strip by Johnny B. Gruelle.
Distributor: Paramount
In *Paramount-Bray Pictographs*

1917
(1)   Feb. 18   *Quacky Doodles' Picnic*
(2)   March 12   *Quacky Doodles' Food Crisis*
(3)   April 1   *Quacky Doodles the Early Bird*
(4)   April 23   *Quacky Doodles Soldiering for Fair*
(5)   Sept. 10   *Quacky Doodles Signs the Pledge*
(6)   Oct. 15   *Quacky Doodles the Cheater*

66.   Picto Puzzles

Bray Productions
Producer: John R. Bray
Director/Story/Animation: Sam Lloyd
Distributor: Paramount
In *Paramount-Bray Pictographs*

1917
(1)   April 2   No. 1
(2)   April 16   No. 2
(3)   May 14   No. 3
(4)   May 21   No. 4
(5)   July 2   No. 5
(6)   July 30   No. 6
(7)   Aug. 27   No. 7

67. *Gaumont Reel Life*

Gaumont Co.
"Technical Cartoons": items in a weekly magazine film series.

1917

(1) April 5   *A One Man Submarine*
(2) April 12   *A Flying Torpedo*
(3) April 26   *Cargo Boats of Tomorrow*
(4) June 7   *The Liberty Loan*

68. *Universal Screen Magazine*

Universal Pictures
Producer: Carl Laemmle

1917

(1) April 20   *Trench Warfare in the Sahara*
               Animator: J.R. Williams

1918

(2) June 29   *Hy Mayer Cartoon*
(3) July 27   *Hy Mayer Cartoon*
(4) Aug. 3   *Hy Mayer Cartoon*
(5) Sept. 1   *Hy Mayer Cartoon*
(6) Oct. 12   *Hy Mayer Cartoon*
(7) Oct. 19   *Hy Mayer Cartoon*
(8) Oct. 26   *Hy Mayer Cartoon*

1919

(9) Jan. 18   *Hy Mayer Cartoon*
(10)   *The Praying Mantis*
               Animator: Leslie Elton
(11)   *War in the Air*
               Animator: Leslie Elton
(12)   *Won't You Walk into My Parlor*
               Animator: Leslie Elton
(13)   *Nightmare Experiences After a Heavy Supper*
               Animator: Leslie Elton
(14)   *How Many Bars in a Beetle's Beat*
               Animator: Leslie Elton

(15)		*The Sea Serpent and the Flying Dragon*
		Animator: Leslie Elton
(16)		*The Courteous Cries of a Cricket*
		Animator: Leslie Elton
(17)		*The Lays of an Ostrich Eggstrawdinary*
		Animator: Leslie Elton
(18)		*Aphides the Animated Ant's Avarice*
		Animator: Leslie Elton
(19)		*The Heart Bug*
		Animator: Leslie Elton
(20)		*The Male Mosquito*
		Animator: Leslie Elton
(21)		*Oft in the Stilly Night*
		Animator: Leslie Elton
(22)		*Ginger for Pluck*
		Animator: Leslie Elton
(23)		*Leading Him a Dance*
		Animator: Leslie Elton
(24)	Dec. 6	*Cinema Luke*
		Animator: Leslie Elton

1920

(25)	March 11	*Cinema Luke*
		Animator: Leslie Elton
(26)	May 6	*It's a Bear*
		Animator: Leslie Elton
(27)	May 28	*Cinema Luke*
		Animator: Leslie Elton

69.　*Paul Terry Feature Burlesques*

Producer/Director/Story: Paul Terry
Distributor: A. Kay Company

1917

(1)	April 23	*20,000 Feats Under the Sea*
(2)	April 30	*Golden Spoon Mary*
(3)	July	*Some Barrier*
(4)	July	*His Trial*

70. Otto Luck

Bray Productions
Producer: John R. Bray
Director/Story/Animation: Wallace A. Carlson
Distributor: Paramount

In *Paramount-Bray Pictographs*

1917

(1)	June 4	*Otto Luck in the Movies*
(2)	June 25	*Otto Luck to the Rescue*
(3)	July 16	*Otto Luck and the Ruby of Razmataz*
(4)	Aug. 13	*Otto Luck's Flivvered Romance*

71. Terry Human Interest Reels

Paul Terry
Producer/Director: Paul Terry
Story: Jessie Allen Fowler
Distributor: A. Kay Company

1917

(1)	June	*Character as Revealed by the Nose*
(2)	July	*Character as Revealed by the Eye*
(3)	Aug.	*Character as Revealed by the Mouth*
(4)	Sept.	*Character as Revealed by the Ear*

72. Leaves from Life

Gaumont Co.
Cartoons from *Life* magazine.
Animated sequences for magazine film series.
In *Reel Life*

1917

(1)	July 5	No. 62
(2)	July 12	No. 63 (A Hasty Pudding)
(3)	July 19	No. 64

(4)	July 26	No. 65
(5)	Aug. 2	No. 66
(6)	Aug. 9	No. 67 (Not a Shadow of a Doubt)
(7)	Aug. 16	No. 68 (The Absent Minded Dentist)
(8)	Aug. 23	No. 69
(9)	Aug. 30	No. 70 (The March of Science)
(10)	Sept. 6	No. 71 (Fresh Advances)
(11)	Sept. 20	No. 73 (When a Big Car Goes By)
(12)	Sept. 27	No. 74 (So Easy)
(13)	Oct. 4	No. 75
(14)	Oct. 11	No. 76
(15)	Oct. 18	No. 77
(16)	Oct. 25	No. 78
(17)	Oct. 31	No. 79 (Had Your Missing Stock Panned Out)
(18)	Nov. 8	No. 80 (It Was Not the Colic)

73. *Abie the Agent*

International Film Service
Producer: William Randolph Hearst
Director: Gregory La Cava
Based on the comic strip by Harry Hershfield.

1917

(1)	Aug. 5	*Iska Worreh*
(2)	Sept. 23	*Abie Kabibble Outwitting His Rival*

74. *Rhyme Reels*

Filmcraft Corporation
Producer/Director/Story: Walt Mason
Live action with animated sequences.

1917

(1)	Aug. 18	*Bunked and Paid For*
(2)	Aug. 18	*The Dipper*
(3)	Aug.	*True Love and Fake Money*
(4)	Aug.	*Hash*

75. *Goodrich Dirt*

Bray Productions
Producer: John R. Bray
Director/Story/Animation: Wallace A. Carlson
Distributor: Paramount

In *Paramount-Bray Pictograph*

1917
  (1) Sept. 3   *Goodrich Dirt at the Seashore*
                          reissue: *Goodrich Dirt Among the Beach Nuts*
  (2) Oct. 1   *Goodrich Dirt Lunch Detective*
  (3) Nov. 5   *Goodrich Dirt at the Training Camp*
  (4) Dec. 2   *Goodrich Dirt's Amateur Night*
                          reissue: *Goodrich Dirt at the Amateur Show*
  (5) Dec. 23 *Goodrich Dirt and the $1,000 Reward*

1918
  (6) Jan. 6   *Goodrich Dirt and the Duke de Whatanob*
  (7) Feb. 11   *Goodrich Dirt's Bear Hunt*
                          reissue: *Goodrich Dirt's Bear Facts*
  (8) March 18 *Goodrich Dirt in the Barber Business*
  (9) April 6   *Goodrich Dirt Mat Artist*
 (10) May 6   *Goodrich Dirt Bad Man Tamer*
 (11) May 27   *Goodrich Dirt in Darkest Africa*
 (12) June 17 *Goodrich Dirt King of Spades*
 (13) July 8   *Goodrich Dirt the Cop*
 (14) Aug. 5   *Goodrich Dirt the Dark and Stormy Knight*
 (15) Aug. 26 *Goodrich Dirt Coin Collector*
 (16) Sept. 30 *Goodrich Dirt Millionaire*
 (17) Oct. 29 *Goodrich Dirt When Wishes Come True*
 (18) Dec. 4   *Goodrich Dirt Cowpuncher*

1919
 (19) Jan. 6   *Goodrich Dirt in Spot Goes Romeoing*
 (20) Jan. 22   *Goodrich Dirt in a Difficult Delivery*
 (21) Feb. 26 *Goodrich Dirt Hypnotist*

76.　*Universal Current Events*

Universal Pictures
Producer: Carl Laemmle
Animated versions of newspaper cartoons as items in a weekly
　newsreel.

1917

(1)　Oct. 13　*Cartoons*
　　　　　　　"On the Way" by Siebel; "Test of Patriotism"
　　　　　　　　by Brown; "Hoch der Sedition" by Greene

1918

(2)　　　　　　*Hoch der Kaiser*
　　　　　　　Animator: Leslie Elton
(3)　　　　　　*Liberty On Guard*
　　　　　　　Animator: Leslie Elton
(4)　　　　　　*Doing Their Bit*
　　　　　　　Animator: Leslie Elton
(5)　Sept. 28　*Cartoon*
　　　　　　　Animator: Arthur Lewis
　　　　　　　(NB: No further titles traced.)

77.　*Merkel Cartoons*

Merkel Film Co.
Producer: Arno Merkel
Director/Story/Animation: Kenneth M. Anderson

1918

(1)　Feb.　*Me and Gott*
(2)　Feb.　*Power Pro and Con*
(3)　April　*The Girth of a Nation*
(4)　April　*Truths on the War in Slang*
(5)　April　*Oh What a Beautiful Dream*
(6)　April　*Hocking the Kaiser*

78.　*Out of the Inkwell*

Bray Productions

Producer: John R. Bray
Director: Dave Fleischer
Animator/Story: Max Fleischer

Paramount-Bray Pictographs
Distributor: Paramount Famous-Lasky

1918
(1) June 10   *Experiment No. 1*

1919
(2) March 5   *Experiment No. 2*
(3) April 2   *Experiment No. 3*

Goldwyn-Bray Pictographs

1919
(4) Aug. 30   *The Clown's Pup*
(5) Oct. 4   *The Tantalizing Fly*
(6) Dec. 3   *Slides*

1920
(7) Feb. 2   *The Boxing Kangaroo*
(8) March 19 *The Chinaman*
(9) May 6   *The Circus*
(10) June 4   *The Ouija Board*
(11) July 6   *The Clown's Little Brother*
(12) Oct. 2   *Poker*
                reissue: *The Card Game*
(13) Oct. 2   *Perpetual Motion*
(14) Nov. 6   *The Restaurant*

1921
(15) Feb. 2   *Cartoonland*
(16) June 20 *The Automobile Ride*

Out of the Inkwell Films Inc.
Distributor: Winkler Pictures
Producer: Max Fleischer
Director: Dave Fleischer
Animators: Max Fleischer, Dick Huemer, Roland Crandall, Art
  Davis, Burton Gillett

1921
  (17)   Oct.   *Modelling*
  (18)   Nov. 21   *Fishing*
  (19)   Dec. 3   *Invisible Ink*

1922
  Distributor: Warner Bros.
  (20)   Jan. 7   *The Fish*
  (21)   Feb. 7   *The Dresden Doll*
                     aka: *The Dancing Doll*
  (22)   March 6   *The Mosquito*

  Distributor: Winkler Pictures
  (23)   April 20   *Bubbles*
  (24)   May   *Flies*
  (25)   July 8   *Pay Day*
  (26)   July 26   *The Hypnotist*
  (27)   Aug. 29   *The Challenge*
  (28)   Sept. 21   *The Show*
  (29)   Oct. 27   *The Reunion*
  (30)   Nov. 4   *The Birthday*
  (31)   Dec. 15   *Jumping Beans*

  Distributor: Rodner Productions
1923
  (32)   Feb. 3   *Modeling*
  (33)   March 15   *Surprise*
  (34)   April 15   *The Puzzle*
  (35)   May 15   *Trapped*
  (36)   July 1   *The Battle*
  (37)   Aug. 1   *False Alarm*
  (38)   Sept. 1   *Balloons*
  (39)   Oct. 1   *The Fortune Teller*
  (40)   Nov. 1   *Shadows*
  (41)   Dec. 1   *Bed Time*

1924
  Distributor: Red Seal Pictures Corp.
  (42)   Jan. 1   *The Laundry*

(43)	Feb. 1	*Masquerade*
(44)	Feb. 21	*The Cartoon Factory*
(45)	March 21	*Mother Gooseland*
(46)	April 1	*A Trip to Mars*
(47)	May 1	*A Stitch in Time*
(48)	May 28	*Clay Town*
(49)	June 25	*The Runaway*
(50)	July 23	*Vacation*
(51)	Aug. 20	*Vaudeville*
(52)	Sept. 17	*League of Nations*
(53)	Oct.	*Sparring Partners*
(54)	Dec. 13	*The Cure*

1925

(55)	Jan.	*Koko the Hot Shot*
(56)	Feb. 25	*Koko the Barber*
(57)	March 2	*Big Chief Koko*
(58)	March 21	*The Storm*
(59)	May 9	*Koko Trains 'Em*
		aka: *Koko Trains Animals*
(60)	June 13	*Koko Sees Spooks*
(61)	July 4	*Koko Celebrates the Fourth*
(62)	Sept. 5	*Koko Nuts*
(63)	Sept. 26	*Koko on the Run*
(64)	Oct. 17	*Koko Packs 'Em*
		aka: *Koko Packs Up*
(65)	Nov. 15	*Koko Eats*
(66)	Nov. 21	*Koko's Thanksgiving*
(67)	Nov. 21	*Koko Steps Out*
(68)	Dec. 12	*Koko in Toyland*

1926

(69)	Feb. 27	*Koko's Paradise*
(70)	March 6	*Koko Baffles the Bulls*
(71)	May 1	*It's the Cats*
(72)	May 1	*Koko at the Circus*
(73)	June 5	*Toot Toot*
(74)	June 12	*Koko Hot After It*
(75)	Sept. 1	*The Fadeaway*
(76)	Oct. 1	*Koko's Queen*

(77) Oct.   *Koko Kidnapped*
(78) Nov. 1   *Koko the Convict*
(79) Dec. 1   *Koko Gets Egg-cited*

1927
(80) Jan. 1   *Koko Back Tracks*
(81) Feb. 10   *Koko Makes 'Em Laugh*
(82) March 10   *Koko in 1999*
(83) April 10   *Koko the Kavalier*
(84) May 10   *Koko Needles the Boss*

series continued under the new title of **The Inkwell Imps.**

79. B.D.F. Cartoons

B.D.F. Film Co.
Producers: Bosworth, Joseph DeFrenes, Paul M. Felton
Director/Animation: Paul M. Felton
Advertising cartoons for various sponsors.
(NB: Many titles untraced.)

1918
(1) July 13   *Old Tire Man Diamond Cartoon Film*

1919
(2) Sept. 10 *Re-blazing the '49 Trail in a Motor Car Train*
(3) Sept. 13 *Tire Injury*
(4) Sept. 13 *Paradental Anesthesia*

1921
(5) Dec. 17   *A Movie Trip Through Film Land*

1922
(6) Nov. 20   *For Any Occasion*
(7) Nov. 20   *In Hot Weather*

1923
(8) Sept. 30 *The Champion* (239)
(9) Nov. 1   *Land of the Unborn Children*

1924
(10)   *Some Impressions on the Subject of Thrift*

1925

(11) May 22   *Live and Help Live*

1926

(12) June 15   *The Carriage Awaits*
(13) June 15   *Family Album*
(14) June 16   *What Price Noise*
(15) Dec. 30   *For Dear Life*
          Story: Paul Barnett

80. *Judge Rummy*

aka: *Silk Hat Harry's Divorce Suit*
International Film Service
Producer: William Randolph Hearst
Director: Gregory La Cava
Animation: Gregory La Cava, Grim Natwick, Jack King, Burton Gillett, Frank Moser, Isadore Klein
Based on the comic strip by Thomas "Tad" Dorgan.

1918

(1) Aug. 19   *Judge Rummy's Off Day* (500)
          GB: *His Day Off*
          Director: Gregory La Cava
(2) Oct.   *Hash and Hypnotism* (670)
(3) Dec.   *Twinkle Twinkle* (575)

1919

(4) March 22 *Snappy Cheese* (570)
(5) June 22   *The Sawdust Trail* (500)
(6) June 29   *The Breath of a Nation*
(7) Aug. 24   *Good Night Nurse*
(8) Sept.   *Judge Rummy's Miscue* (550)
(9) Oct.   *Rubbing It In* (475)
(10) Nov.   *A Sweet Pickle* (450)

changed to **Goldwyn-Bray Comic**

1920

(11) April 21   *Shimmie Shivers*

(12) May 7   *A Fitting Gift*
(13) May 25   *His Last Legs*
(14) June 6   *Smokey Smokes*
             Director: Gregory La Cava
(15) June 19   *Doctors Should Have Patience*
(16) July 3   *A Fish Story*
(17) July 17   *The Last Rose of Summer*
(18) Aug. 26   *The Fly Guy*
(19) Sept. 5   *Shedding the Profiteer*
(20) Sept. 22   *The Sponge Man*
(21) Oct. 3   *The Prize Dance*

changed to *International Cartoons*

1920
(22) Oct. 26   *Hypnotic Hooch*
             Director: Grim Natwick
(23) Nov. 3   *The Hooch Ball*
(24) Nov. 3   *Kiss Me*
             Director: Jack King
(25) Nov. 22   *Snap Judgement*
             Director: Burton Gillett
(26) Nov. 22   *Why Change Your Husband*
             Director: Jack King
(27) Dec. 10   *Bear Facts*
             Director: Gregory La Cava
(28) Dec. 12   *Yes Dear*
             Director: Grim Natwick

1921
(29) Jan. 4   *Too Much Pep*
             Director: Jack King
(30) Jan. 17   *The Chicken Thief*
             Director: Grim Natwick
(31) March 15   *The Skating Fool*

81. *Charlie*

Nestor Films/Universal Pictures

Producer/Director: Pat Sullivan
Animation: Otto Messmer
Distributor: Universal

1918

(1)	Sept. 3	*How Charlie Captured the Kaiser* (1000)
		GB: *A Modern Bill Adams* (500)
(2)	and	*Knocking the "I" Out of Kaiser* (500)
		(N.B.: Released as two short films)
(3)	Dec. 21	*Over the Rhine with Charlie* (1000)
		GB: *Just a Few Lines* (500)
(4)	and	*The Whine of the Rhine* (500)
		(NB: Released as two short films)

1919

(5)	Jan. 29	*Charlie in Turkey*
		GB: *Turkish Delight*
(6)	March 24	*Charlie Treats 'Em Rough*
		GB: *Treating 'Em Rough*

82. *Tad Cartoons*

International Film Service
Producer: William Randolph Hearst
Animators: William Nolan, Walter Lantz
Based on the newspaper cartoons by Thomas "Tad" Dorgan.

1918

(1)		*Tad's Little Daffydills*
		Director: Bill Nolan
(2)		*Tad's Indoor Sports*
		Director: Bill Nolan, Walter Lantz

In *International News*
Animated cartoon items in weekly newsreel.

1919

| (3) | April 23 | *Tad Cartoon* |

1920

| (4) | Feb. 21 | *Indoor Sports by Tad* |

83. *Hardrock Dome*

Bray Productions
Producer: John R. Bray
Director: Pat Sullivan
Distributor: Paramount

In *Paramount-Bray Pictographs*

1919
(1)	Jan. 29	Episode 1
(2)	Feb. 5	Episode 2
(3)	Feb. 12	Episode 3

84. *The Whozit Weekly*

Universal Pictures Co.
Producer: Carl Laemmle
Director/Story/Animation: Leslie Elton
Burlesque newsreel item in weekly magazine film series.

In *Universal Screen Magazine*

1919
(1)	March 23	No. 115
(2)	May 18	No. 123
(3)	May 25	No. 124
(4)	June 8	No. 126
(5)	June 29	No. 129
(6)	July 13	No. 131
(7)	Aug. 3	No. 134
(8)	Aug. 24	No. 137
(9)	Oct. 4	No. 143
(10)	Oct. 11	No. 144

1920
(11)	Feb. 28	No. 164

85. *Us Fellers*

Bray Productions
Producer: John R. Bray

Director/Story/Animation: Wallace A. Carlson
Distributor: Paramount

In *Paramount-Bray Pictographs*

1919
- (1) April 12 *Dud Perkins Gets Mortified*
- (2) April 26 *The Parson*
- (3) May 24 *Wounded by the Beauty*
- (4) May 29 *Dud the Circus Performer*
- (5) June 21 *Dud's Greatest Cirkus on Earth*
- (6) Aug. 7 *At the Ol' Swimmin' Hole*

In *Goldwyn-Bray Pictographs*

1919
- (7) Sept. 23 *Dud's Home Run*
- (8) Oct. 9 *Dud Leaves Home*
- (9) Nov. 17 *Dud's Geography Lesson*
- (10) Dec. 31 *A Chip Off the Old Block*

1920
- (11) Feb. 16 *Dud's Haircut*
- (12) Sept. 9 *Dud the Lion Tamer*

86. *Goldwyn-Bray Pictographs*

(Continuation of *Paramount-Bray Pictographs*.)
Bray Productions and
International Film Service (IFS)
Producer: John R. Bray
Directors: Max Fleischer, Gregory La Cava, Raoul Barré, Wallace
A. Carlson, Pat Sullivan, Milt Gross, Leighton Budd, Vernon
Stallings, J.D. Leventhal, F. Lyle Goldman, L.M. Glackens,
Dave Fleischer, Jean Gic
Distributor: Goldwyn Pictures Corporation

1919

  (1)   Aug. 30   *The Clown's Pup*
                     Director: Max Fleischer

  (2)   Sept. 6   *How Animated Cartoons Are Made*
                     Director: John R. Bray

  (3)   Sept. 6   *Where Has My Little Coal Bin* (IFS)
                     Director: Gregory La Cava
                     (*Jerry on the Job*)

  (4)   Sept. 13   *The High Cost of Living* (IFS)
                     Director: Raoul Barré

  (5)   Sept. 23   *Dud's Home Run*
                     Director: Wallace Carlson
                     (*Us Fellers*)

  (6)   Sept. 27   *Getting a Story or the Origin of the Shimmie*
                     Director: Pat Sullivan

  (7)   Oct. 4   *Useless Hints by Fuller Prunes*
                     Director/Story: Milt Gross

  (8)   Oct. 4   *The Tantalizing Fly*
                     Director: Max Fleischer

  (9)   Oct. 9   *Dud Leaves Home*
                     Director: Wallace Carlson
                     (*Us Fellers*)

  (10)   Oct. 25   *My How Times Have Changed*
                     Director: Leighton Budd

  (11)   Nov. 7   *We'll Say They Do*
                     Director/Story: Milt Gross

  (12)   Nov. 10   *Pigs in Clover* (IFS)
                     Director: Gregory La Cava

  (13)   Nov. 17   *Dud's Geography Lesson*
                     Director: Wallace Carlson
                     (*Us Fellers*)

  (14)   Nov. 26   *How Could William Tell* (IFS)
                     Director: Gregory La Cava

  (15)   Dec. 3   *Slides*
                     Director: Max Fleischer

  (16)   Dec. 9   *Sauce for the Goose* (IFS)
                     Director: Vernon Stallings

  (17)   Dec. 16   *Tumult in Toy Town*
                     Director/Story: Milt Gross

(18) Dec. 23   *Sufficiency* (IFS)
               Director: Vernon Stallings
(19) Dec. 31   *A Chip Off the Old Block*
               Director: Wallace Carlson
               (*Us Fellers*)

1920
(20) Jan. 6   *The Chinese Question* (IFS)
               Director: Vernon Stallings
(21) Jan. 16   *The Great Cheese Robbery* (IFS)
               (*Krazy Kat*)
(22) Jan. 16   *Behind the Signs on Broadway*
               Director: J.D. Leventhal
(23) Jan. 26   *The Debut of Thomas Katt*
               Director: John R. Bray
               (N.B.: The first color cartoon film made in
                  Brewster Color.)
(24) Jan. 30   *Love's Labor Lost* (IFS)
               Director: Vernon Stallings
               (*Krazy Kat*)
(25) Feb. 2   *The Boxing Kangaroo*
               Director: Max Fleischer
(26) Feb. 10   *A Warm Reception* (IFS)
               (*Jerry on the Job*)
(27) Feb. 10   *All Aboard for a Trip to the Moon*
               Director: Max Fleischer
(28) Feb. 16   *Dud's Haircut*
               Director: Wallace Carlson
               (*Us Fellers*)
(29) Feb. 16   *How You See*
               Director: J.D. Leventhal
(30) Feb. 27   *The Wrong Track* (IFS)
               (*Jerry on the Job*)
(31) Feb. 27   *Wireless Telephony*
               Director: F. Lyle Goldman
(32) March 3   *The Best Mouse Loses* (IFS)
               Director: Vernon Stallings
               (*Krazy Kat*)
(33) March 3   *Hello Mars*

Director: Max Fleischer

(34) March 9 *The Tale of a Wag* (IFS)
(*Jerry on the Job*)

(35) March 9 *Professor B. Flat*

Director: J.D. Leventhal, R.D. Crandall

(36) March 19 *The Chinaman*

Director: Max Fleischer

(37) March 23 *A Very Busy Day* (IFS)

Director: Gregory La Cava
(*Jerry on the Job*)

(38) April 3 *Frenchy Discovers America*

Director/Story: Milt Gross

(39) April 14 *A Tax from the Rear* (IFS)
(*Krazy Kat*)

(40) April 14 *The Ear*

Director: F. Lyle Goldman

(41) April 21 *Spring Fever* (IFS)

Director: Gregory La Cava
(*Jerry on the Job*)

(42) April 30 *Ginger Snaps*

Director/Story: Milt Gross

(43) May 6 *The Circus*

Director: Dave Fleischer

(44) May 14 *Swinging His Vacation* (IFS)

Director: Gregory La Cava
(*Jerry on the Job*)

(45) May 14 *Here's Your Eyesight*

Director: J.D. Leventhal

(46) May 19 *Yes Times Have Changed*

Director: L.M. Glackens

(47) May 29 *The Mysterious Vamp* (IFS)

Director: Gregory La Cava
(*Jerry on the Job*)

(48) June 4 *Katz Is Katz* (IFS)

Director: Vernon Stallings
(*Krazy Kat*)

(49) June 4 *The Ouija Board*

Director: Dave Fleischer

(50) June 12 *A Punk Piper* (IFS)

Director: Vernon Stallings
(*Jerry on the Job*)

(51) June 12   *Breathing*
Director: J.D. Leventhal

(52) June 19   *How My Vacation Spent Me*
Director/Story: Milt Gross
(*Ginger Snaps*)

(53) June 26   *Quick Change* (IFS)
Director: Vernon Stallings
(*Jerry on the Job*)

(54) July 3   *The Chinese Honeymoon* (IFS)
(*Krazy Kat*)

(55) July 6   *The Clown's Little Brother*
Director: Dave Fleischer

(56) July 16   *The Rhyme that Went Wrong* (IFS)
Director: Vernon Stallings
(*Jerry on the Job*)

(57) July 27   *The Trained Horse* (IFS)
Director: Vernon Stallings
(*Jerry on the Job*)

(58) Aug. 26   *Dots and Dashes* (IFS)
Director: Vernon Stallings
(*Jerry on the Job*)

(59) Aug. 26   *The Train Robber* (IFS)
Director: Vernon Stallings
(*Jerry on the Job*)

(60) Aug. 26   *If You Could Shrink*
Director: Dave Fleischer

(61) Sept. 4   *Dud the Lion Tamer*
Director/Story: Wallace Carlson
(*Us Fellers*)

(62) Sept. 11   *Water Water Everywhere* (IFS)
Director: Vernon Stallings
(*Jerry on the Job*)

(63) Sept. 18   *Ze American Girl*
Director/Story: Jean Gic

(64) Sept. 25   *Ginger Snaps*
Director/Story: Milt Gross

(65) Sept. 25   *If We Went to the Moon*

Director: J.D. Leventhal
(66) Oct. 2 *Poker*
Director: Dave Fleischer
(67) Oct. 2 *Jerry and the Five Fifteen Train* (IFS)
Director: Vernon Stallings
(*Jerry on the Job*)
(68) Oct. 2 *Lightning*
Director: J.D. Leventhal
(69) Oct. 2 *Perpetual Motion*
Director: Dave Fleischer
(70) Oct. 7 *Beaten by a Hare* (IFS)
Director: Vernon Stallings
(*Jerry on the Job*)
(71) Oct. 7 *A Tough Pull* (IFS)
Director: Vernon Stallings
(*Jerry on the Job*)
(72) Oct. 21 *Stories in Lines*
Director/Story: Jean Gic
(73) Oct. 25 *A Family Affair* (IFS)
(*Krazy Kat*)
(74) Nov. 2 *A Continuous Line of Thought*
Director/Story: Jean Gic
(75) Nov. 6 *The Bomb Idea* (IFS)
Director: Vernon Stallings
(*Jerry on the Job*)
(76) Nov. 16 *The Restaurant*
Director: Dave Fleischer
(77) Dec. 14 *A Thrilling Drill* (IFS)
Director: Vernon Stallings
(*Jerry on the Job*)

1921
(78) Jan. 8 *The Hinges on the Bar Room Door* (IFS)
Director: Vernon Stallings
(79) Jan. 8 *Without Coal* (IFS)
Director: Vernon Stallings
(*Jerry on the Job*)
(80) Jan. 8 *The Automatic Riveter*
Director: J.D. Leventhal

(81)	Jan. 15	*A Tragedy in One Line*
		Director/Story: Jean Gic
(82)	Jan. 21	*The Awful Spook* (IFS)
(83)	Jan. 26	*How I Became Krazy* (IFS)
		Director: Vernon Stallings
		(*Krazy Kat*)
(84)	Jan. 28	*Scrambled Eagles* (IFS)
		Director: Vernon Stallings
		(*Krazy Kat*)
(85)	Feb. 2	*Cartoonland*
		Director: Dave Fleischer
(86)	Feb. 12	*The Automobile Ride*
		Director: Dave Fleischer
(87)	Feb. 16	*Izzy Able the Detective*
		Director/Story: Milt Gross
(88)	Feb. 26	*The Wireless Wire Walkers* (IFS)
		(*Krazy Kat*)
(89)	March 19	*Othello Sapp's Wonderful Invention*
		reissue: *The Cow Milker*
		Director/Story: Milt Gross

87. *Cinema Luke*

Universal Pictures
Producer: Carl Laemmle
Director/Story/Animation: Leslie Elton
Combined live action and animation.
In *Universal Screen Magazine*

1919

(1)	Dec. 6	*Cinema Luke*

1920

(2)	March 11	*Cinema Luke*
(3)	May 28	*Cinema Luke*
		(NB: Further cartoons in this series untraced.)

88. *International News*

International Film Service

Producer: William Randolph Hearst

1919–1920

Series of animated cartoon items included in the weekly newsreel. Titles untraced, but cartoonists included Hal Coffman, Thomas (Tad) Dorgan, Tom Powers, Frederick Opper, Harry Murphy, Winsor McCay.

89. *Screen Follies*

Capital Film Co.
Producer/Director/Story/Animation: Luis Seel, F.A. Dahme

1920

(1)	Jan. 4	No. 1
(2)	Jan. 4	No. 2

(NB: No further issues traced.)

90. *Paramount Magazine*

Distributor: Paramount Pictures
Magazine film series with animated sequences.

1920

(1) March 14 *The Bone of Contention*
    Director: Paul Terry
(2) March 21 *Handy Mandy's Goat*
    Director: Frank Moser
(3) March 28 *Feline Follies*
    Director: Pat Sullivan
(4) April 4 *Bobby Bumps*
    Director: Earl Hurd
(5) April 11 *The Kids Find Candy's Catching*
    Director: Frank Moser
(6) April 18 *Felix the Cat*
    Director: Pat Sullivan
(7) April 25 *Bobby Bumps*
    Director: Earl Hurd
(8) May 2 *Bud Takes the Cake*
    Director: Frank Moser

(9) May 9   *Felix the Cat*
                Director: Pat Sullivan

(10) May 15   *Bobby Bumps*
                Director: Earl Hurd

(11) May 23   *The New Cook's Debut*
                Director: Frank Moser

(12) May 30   *Felix the Cat*
                Director: Pat Sullivan

(13) June 6   *Bobby Bumps*
                Director: Earl Hurd

(14) June 13   *Mice and Money*
                Director: Frank Moser

(15) June 20   *Felix the Cat*
                Director: Pat Sullivan

(16) June 27   *Silly Hoots*
                Director: Henry D. Bailey

(17) July 4   *The Transatlantic Night Express*
                Director: Harry Leonard

(18) July 11   *Bobby Bumps*
                Director: Earl Hurd

(19) July 18   *Felix the Cat*
                Director: Pat Sullivan

(20) July 25   *Down the Mississippi*
                Director: Frank Moser

(21) Aug. 1   *Silly Hoots*
                Director: Henry D. Bailey

(22) Aug. 8   *Bobby Bumps the Cave Man*
                Director: Earl Hurd

(23) Aug. 15   *Play Ball*
                Director: Frank Moser

(24) Aug. 22   *Romance and Rheumatism*
                Director: Frank Moser

(25) Aug. 29   *Felix the Cat*
                Director: Pat Sullivan

(26) Sept. 5   *Bud and Tommy Take a Day Off*
                Director: Frank Moser

(27) Sept. 12   *Silly Hoots*
                Director: Henry D. Bailey

(28) Sept. 19   *Bobby Bumps*

		Director: Earl Hurd
(29)	Sept. 26	*Felix the Cat*
		Director: Pat Sullivan
(30)	Oct. 3	*The North Pole*
		Director: Frank Moser
(31)	Oct. 10	*Silly Hoots*
		Director: Henry D. Bailey
(32)	Oct. 27	*Bobby Bumps*
		Director: Earl Hurd
(33)	Oct. 24	*Felix the Landlord*
		Director: Pat Sullivan
(34)	Oct. 31	*The Great Clean-Up*
		Director: Frank Moser
(35)	Nov. 7	*A Double Life*
		Director: Henry D. Bailey
(36)	Nov. 14	*Bobby Bumps*
		Director: Earl Hurd
(37)	Nov. 21	*Felix the Cat*
		Director: Pat Sullivan
(38)	and	*One Hundred Percent Proof*
		Director: Harry Leonard
(39)	Nov. 28	*Bud and Susie Join the Tecs*
		Director: Frank Moser
(40)	Dec. 5	*Fifty-Fifty*
		Director: Frank Moser
(41)	Dec. 12	*Silly Hoots*
		Director: Henry D. Bailey
(42)	Dec. 19	*Bobby Bumps' Orchestra*
		Director: Earl Hurd
(43)	Dec. 26	*My Hero*
		Director: Pat Sullivan

1921

(44)	Jan. 2	*Getting Theirs*
		Director: Frank Moser
(45)	and	*Some Sayings of Benjamin Franklin*
		Director: Harry Leonard
(46)	Jan. 9	*Silly Hoots*
		Director: Henry D. Bailey

(47)	Jan. 16	*Bobby Bumps*
		Director: Earl Hurd
(48)	Jan. 23	*Felix the Cat*
		Director: Pat Sullivan
(49)	Jan. 30	*Bud and Susie*
		Director: Frank Moser
(50)	Feb. 6	*Hootch and Mootch in a Steak at Stake*
		Director: Earl Hurd
(51)	and	*Shimmy Geography*
(52)	Feb. 13	*Felix the Cat*
		Director: Pat Sullivan
(53)	Feb. 20	*Bobby Bumps*
		Director: Earl Hurd
(54)	Feb. 27	*Clean Your Feet*
		Director: Frank Moser
(55)	March 6	*Cabaret Courtesy*
		Director: Henry D. Bailey
(56)	March 13	*Bobby Bumps*
		Director: Earl Hurd
(57)	March 20	*Bobby Bumps Checkmated*
		Director: Earl Hurd
(58)	and	*Felix the Hypnotist*
		Director: Pat Sullivan
(59)	and	*The Sheriff*
		Director: Harry Leonard
(60)	March 27	*Silly Hoots*
		Director: Henry D. Bailey
(61)	April 3	*Circumstantial Evidence*
		Director: Frank Moser
(62)	April 10	*Bobby Bumps*
		Director: Earl Hurd
(63)	April 17	*Felix the Cat: Free Lunch*
		Director: Pat Sullivan
		In Greenwich Village
(64)	April 24	*Silly Hoots*
		Director: Henry D. Bailey
(65)	May 1	*Bud and Susie*
		Director: Frank Moser

continued as *Paramount Cartoons*

91.   *Bud and Susie*

Bray Studios
Producer: John R. Bray
Director/Story/Animation: Frank Moser

In *Paramount Magazine*

1920

(1)	March 21	*Handy Mandy's Goat*
(2)	April 11	*The Kids Find Candy's Catching*
(3)	May 2	*Bud Takes the Cake*
(4)	May 23	*The New Cook's Debut*
(5)	June 13	*Mice and Money*
(6)	July 25	*Down the Mississippi*
(7)	Aug. 15	*Play Ball*
(8)	Aug. 29	*Romance and Rheumatism*
(9)	Sept. 5	*Bud and Tommy Take a Day Off*
(10)	Oct. 3	*The North Pole*
(11)	Oct. 31	*The Great Clean Up*
(12)	Nov. 28	*Bud and Susie Join the Tecs*
(13)	Dec. 5	*Fifty-Fifty*

1921

(14)	Jan. 2	*Getting Theirs*
(15)	Feb. 27	*Ma's Wipe Your Feet Campaign*
(16)	April 3	*Circumstantial Evidence*

continued in *Paramount Cartoons*

(17)	May 29	*By the Sea*
(18)	June 26	*$10,000 Under a Pillow*
(19)	July 31	*Dashing North*
(20)	Aug. 28	*Kitchen, Bedroom and Bath*
(21)	Sept.	*The Wars of Mice and Men*

92.   *Felix the Cat*

Pat Sullivan Comics
Producer/Director: Pat Sullivan

Animation: Otto Messmer, Raoul Barré, Dana Parker, Hal Walker, Al Eugster, Jack Boyle, George Cannata, Tom Byrne, Alfred Thurber

Paramount Magazine
Distributor: Paramount

1920

(1)	March 28	*Feline Follies*
(2)	April 18	(title unknown)
(3)	May 9	(title unknown)
(4)	May 30	(title unknown)
(5)	June 20	(title unknown)
(6)	July 18	(title unknown)
(7)	Aug. 29	(title unknown)
(8)	Sept. 26	(title unknown)
(9)	Oct. 24	*Felix the Landlord*
(10)	Nov. 21	(title unknown)
(11)	Dec. 26	*My Hero*

1921

(12)	Jan. 23	(title unknown)
(13)	Feb. 13	(title unknown)
(14)	March 13	*The Hypnotist*
(15)	April 17	*Free Lunch*

continued in *Paramount Cartoons*

(16)	May 15	*Felix Goes on Strike*
(17)	June 5	*Felix in the Love Punch*
(18)	July 3	*Felix out of Luck*
(19)	July 17	*Felix Left at Home*
(20)	Oct. 30	*Felix the Gay Dog*

continued as *Winkler Productions*

1922

(21)	Jan. 22	*Felix Saves the Day* (650)
(22)	Feb.	*Felix at the Fair*
(23)	March	*Felix Makes Good*
(24)	April	*Felix All at Sea*

(25) May   *Felix in Love*
(26) June   *Felix in the Swim*
(27) Oct. 21   *Felix Fifty-Fifty*
(28) Nov. 25   *Felix Wakes Up*

1923

(29) Jan. 1   *Felix Turns the Tide*
(30) Jan. 15   *Felix on the Trail*
(31) Feb. 1   *Felix Lends a Hand*
(32) March 1   *Felix in the Bone Age*
(33) March 15 *Felix the Ghost Breaker*
(34) April 1   *Felix Wins Out*
(35) April 15   *Felix Tries for Treasure*
(36) May 1   *Felix Revolts*
(37) May 15   *Felix Calms His Conscience*
(38) June 1   *Felix the Globe Trotter*
(39) Sept. 1   *Felix Gets Broadcasted*
(40) Sept. 15   *Felix Strikes It Rich*
(41) Oct. 1   *Felix in Hollywood*
(42) Oct. 15   *Felix in Fairyland*
(43) Nov. 1   *Felix Laughs Last*
(44) Nov. 15   *Felix Fills a Shortage*
(45) Dec. 1   *Felix the Goat Getter*
(46) Dec. 15   *Felix Goes A-Hunting*

1924

(47) Jan 1.   *Felix Out of Luck*
(48) Jan. 15   *Felix Loses Out*
(49) Feb. 1   *Felix Hypes the Hippo*
(50) Feb. 15   *Felix Crosses the Crooks*
(51) April 1   *Felix Tries to Rest*
(52) Aug. 15   *Felix Baffled by Banjos*
(53) Sept. 15   *Felix Pinches the Pole*
(54) Oct. 1   *Felix Puts It Over*
(55) Oct. 15   *Felix a Friend in Need*

1925

(56) Jan. 1   *Felix Wins and Loses*
(57) Jan. 15   *Felix All Puzzled*
(58) Feb. 1   *Felix Follows the Swallows*

(59) Feb. 15 *Felix Rests in Peace*
(60) March 1 *Felix Gets His Fill*
(61) April 13 *Felix Full of Fight*
(62) April 27 *Felix Outwits Cupid*
(63) May 8 *Felix Monkeys with Magic*
(64) May 25 *Felix Cops the Prize*
(65) June 8 *Felix Gets the Can*

continued as **Pat Sullivan Productions: Bijou Films**
Distributor: Educational Pictures

1925

(66) Aug. 23 *Felix Trifles with Time*
(67) Sept. 6 *Felix Busts into Business*
(68) Sept. 20 *Felix Trips Thru Toyland*
(69) Oct. 4 *Felix on the Farm*
(70) Oct. 18 *Felix on the Job*
(71) Nov. 1 *Felix in the Cold Rush*
(72) Nov. 15 *Felix in Eats Are West*
(73) Nov. 29 *Felix Tries the Trades*
(74) Dec. 13 *Felix at Rainbow's End*
(75) Dec. 27 *Felix Kept on Walking*

1926

(76) Jan. 30 *Felix Spots the Spook*
(77) March 2 *Felix Flirts with Fate*
(78) March 7 *Felix in Blunderland*
(79) March 20 *Felix Fans the Flames*
(80) March 20 *Felix Laughs It Off*
(81) March 20 *Felix Weathers the Weather*
(82) May 1 *Felix Uses His Head*
(83) May 8 *Felix Misses the Cue*
(84) June 12 *Felix Braves the Briny*
(85) June 26 *Felix in a Tale of Two Kitties*
(86) July 3 *Felix Scoots Thru Scotland*
(87) July 17 *Felix Rings the Ringer*
(88) July 24 *Felix in School Daze*
(89) Aug. 8 *Felix in Gym Gems*
(90) Aug. 8 *Felix Seeks Solitude*
(91) Aug. 22 *Felix in Two-lip Time*

(92)	Aug. 28	*Felix Misses His Swiss*
(93)	Sept. 5	*Felix in Scrambled Yeggs*
(94)	Sept. 19	*Felix Shatters the Sheik*
(95)	Nov. 8	*Felix Hunts the Hunter*
(96)	Nov. 14	*Felix in Reverse English*
(97)	Nov. 19	*Felix in Land o' Fancy*
(98)	Nov. 28	*Felix Trumps the Ace*
(99)	Nov. 30	*Felix Busts a Bubble*
(100)	Dec. 12	*Felix Collars the Button*
(101)	Dec. 26	*Felix in Zoo Logic*

1927

(102)	Jan. 18	*Felix Dines and Pines*
(103)	Feb. 2	*Felix in Icy Eyes*
(104)	Feb. 8	*Felix in Pedigreedy*
(105)	Feb. 20	*Felix Stars in Stripes*
(106)	March 6	*Felix Sees 'Em in Season*
(107)	March 20	*Felix in Barn Yarns*
(108)	April 4	*Felix in Germ Mania*
(109)	April 17	*Felix in Sax Appeal*
(110)	May 1	*Felix in Eye Jinks*
(111)	May 15	*Felix as Roameow*
(112)	May 29	*Felix Ducks His Duty*
(113)	June 12	*Felix in Dough Nutty*
(114)	June 26	*Felix in a Loco Motive*
(115)	July 27	*Felix in Art for Heart's Sake*
(116)	Aug. 10	*Felix in the Travel-hog*
(117)	Aug. 17	*Felix in Jack from All Trades*
(118)	Sept. 20	*Felix in Non Stop Fright*
(119)	Nov. 3	*Felix in Flim Flam Films*
(120)	Nov. 7	*Felix Switches Witches*
(121)	Nov. 16	*Felix in No Fuellin'*
(122)	Nov. 16	*Felix in Wise Guise*
(123)	Nov. 28	*Felix in Daze and Knights*
(124)	Nov. 28	*Felix in Uncle Tom's Crabbin'*
(125)	Dec. 12	*Felix Behind in Front*
(126)	Dec. 19	*Felix Hits the Deck*
(127)	Dec. 27	*Felix in Whys and Other-whys*

1928

(128)	Jan. 8	*Felix in the Smoke Scream*
(129)	Jan. 22	*Felix in Draggin' the Dragon*
(130)	Feb. 5	*Felix in the Oily Bird*
(131)	Feb. 19	*Felix in Ohm Sweet Ohm*
(132)	March 4	*Felix in Japanicky*
(133)	March 18	*Felix in Polly-tics*
(134)	April 15	*Felix in Sure Locked Homes*
(135)	April 29	*Felix in Eskimotive*
(136)	May 7	*Felix in Comicalamities*
(137)	May 13	*Felix in Arabiantics*
(138)	May 27	*Felix in In and Outlaws*
(139)	June 10	*Felix in Outdoor Indore*
(140)	June 24	*Felix in Futuritzy*
(141)	July 8	*Felix in Astronomeows*
(142)	July 22	*Felix in Jungle Bungles*
(143)	Aug. 5	*Felix in the Last Life*

93. *The Shenanigan Kids*

International Film Service/Goldwyn-Bray Comic
Producer: William Randolph Hearst
Director: Gregory La Cava, Burton Gillett, Grim Natwick
Based on the comic strip by Rudolph Dirks.
(Continuation of *The Katzenjammer Kids*.)

1920

(1)	April 17	*Knock on the Window, the Door Is a Jamb*
(2)	June 17	*One Good Turn Deserves Another*
(3)	June 27	*The Dummy*
(4)	July 24	*The Rotisserie Brothers*
		Director: Grim Natwick
(5)	Oct. 9	*Hunting Big Game*
		Director: Burton Gillett

94. *Lampoons*

Bray Productions
Producer: John R. Bray

Director/Animation: Burton Gillett
Distributor: Goldwyn Pictures
Series of joke cartoons redrawn from the magazines *Judge* and
 Leslie's Weekly.
In *Goldwyn-Bray Comic*

1920
   (1)   April 17– *Lampoons*
          Oct. 9   23 editions with the same title

95. *Goldwyn-Bray Comic*

Bray Studios; International Film Service
Producer: John R. Bray
Directors: Gregory La Cava, Max Fleischer, Burton L. Gillett,
 Grim Natwick
Animators: John Foster, Vernon Stallings, Walter Lantz
Distributor: Goldwyn Pictures Corporation

1920
   (1)   April 17   *The Great Umbrella Mystery*
                    Director: Gregory La Cava
                    (*Happy Hooligan*)
   (2)   April 17   *Knock on the Window, the Door Is a Jamb*
                    (*Shenanigan Kids*)
   (3)   April 21   *Shimmie Shivers*
                    (*Judge Rummy*)
   (4)   April 21   *The First Man to the Moon*
                    Director: Max Fleischer
   (5)   May 7   *A Fitting Gift*
                    (*Judge Rummy*)
   (6)   May 25   *His Last Legs*
                    (*Judge Rummy*)
   (7)   June 2   *Turn to the Right Leg*
                    (*Happy Hooligan*)
   (8)   June 6   *Smokey Smokes*
                    (*Judge Rummy*)
   (9)   June 17   *One Good Turn Deserves Another*
                    (*Shenanigan Kids*)

(10) June 18   *All for the Love of a Girl*
                (*Happy Hooligan*)
(11) June 19   *Doctors Should Have Patience*
                (*Judge Rummy*)
(12) June 27   *The Dummy*
                (*Shenanigan Kids*)
(13) July 3   *His Country Cousin*
                (*Happy Hooligan*)
(14) July 3   *A Fish Story*
                (*Judge Rummy*)
(15) July 10   *Lampoons*
                Director:Burton Gillett
(16) July 17   *The Last Rose of Summer*
                (*Judge Rummy*)
(17) July 24   *The Rotisserie Brothers*
                Director: Grim Natwick
                (*Shenanigan Kids*)
(18) Aug. 26   *The Fly Guy*
                (*Judge Rummy*)
(19) Sept. 5   *Shedding the Profiteer*
                (*Judge Rummy*)
(20) Sept. 11 *Cupid's Advice*
                (*Happy Hooligan*)
(21) Sept. 11 *Happy Houldini*
                (*Happy Hooligan*)
(22) Sept. 18 *Apollo*
                (*Happy Hooligan*)
(23) Sept. 22 *The Sponge Man*
                (*Judge Rummy*)
(24) Oct. 3   *The Prize Dance*
                (*Judge Rummy*)
(25) Oct. 9   *Hunting Big Game*
                (*Shenanigan Kids*)

96. *Ginger Snaps*

Bray Studios
Producer: John R. Bray
Director/Story/Animation: Milt Gross

In *Goldwyn-Bray Pictographs*

1920

  (1) April 30 *Ginger Snaps* (277)
  (2) June 19 *How My Vacation Spent Me* (230)
  (3) Sept. 27 *Ginger Snaps* (182)

97. *The Gumps*

Celebrated Players Film Corporation
Producer/Director: Wallace A. Carlson
Animation: Wallace A. Carlson, David Hand, Bill Roberts, Paul
  Satterfield
Story: from the comic strip by Sidney Smith.

1920

  (1) June 5 *Andy's Dancing Lesson*
  (2) June 5 *Flat Hunting*
  (3) June 5 *Andy Visits His Mamma-in-Law*
  (4) June 26 *Andy Spends a Quiet Day at Home*
  (5) June 26 *Andy Plays Golf*
  (6) June 26 *Andy's Wash Day*
  (7) June 26 *Andy on Skates*
  (8) June 26 *Andy's Mother-in-Law Pays Him a Visit*
  (9) July 3 *Andy on a Diet*
(10) July 3 *Andy's Night Out*
(11) Aug. 14 *Andy and Min at the Theatre*
(12) Aug. 14 *Andy Visits the Osteopath*
(13) Oct. 23 *Andy's Inter-Ruben Guest*
(14) Oct. 23 *Andy Redecorates His Flat*
(15) Oct. 23 *Andy the Model*
(16) Oct. 23 *Accidents Will Happen*
(17) Oct. 23 *Andy Fights the High Cost of Living*
(18) Oct. 23 *Militant Min*
(19) Oct. 23 *Ice Box Episodes*
(20) Oct. 23 *Wim and Wigor*
(21) Oct. 23 *Equestrian Andy*
(22) Oct. 23 *Andy the Hero*
                aka: *Andy Plays Hero*
(23) Oct. 23 *Andy's Picnic*

(24)	Oct. 23	*Andy the Chicken Farmer*
(25)	Oct. 23	*Andy the Actor*
(26)	Oct. 23	*Andy at Shady Rest*
(27)	Oct. 23	*Andy on the Beach*
(28)	Oct. 23	*Andy on Pleasure Bent*
(29)	Oct. 23	*Howdy Partner*
(30)	Nov. 27	*There's a Reason*
(31)	Nov. 27	*Ship Ahoy*
(32)	Nov. 27	*The Toreador*
(33)	Nov. 27	*The Broilers*
(34)	Nov. 27	*Flicker Flicker Little Star*
(35)	Nov. 27	*Mixing Business with Pleasure*
(36)	Nov. 27	*Up She Goes*
(37)	Nov. 27	*Westward Ho*
(38)	Nov. 27	*A-Hunting We Will Go*
(39)	Nov. 27	*Get to Work*

1921

(40)	Feb. 12	*The Best of Luck*
(41)	Feb. 12	*The Promoters*
(42)	Feb. 12	*The Masked Ball*
(43)	Feb. 12	*Give 'Er the Gas*
(44)	Feb. 12	*Chester's Cat*
(45)	Feb. 12	*Rolling Around*
(46)	Feb. 12	*Andy's Holiday*
(47)	Feb. 12	*Andy Has a Caller*
(48)	Feb. 12	*Le Cuspidorée*
		aka: *Il Cuspidore*
(49)	Feb. 26	*Andy's Cow*
(50)	March 19	*Jilted and Jolted*
(51)	March 19	*A Terrible Time*
(52)	May 14	*A Quiet Little Game*
(53)	May 14	*Andy's Dog Day*
(54)	June	*Fatherly Love*
(55)	June	*The Chicken Thief*

98. *Silly Hoots*

Henry D. Bailey
Producer/Director/Story/Animation: Henry D. Bailey

Distributor: Paramount Pictures
In *Paramount Magazine*

1920

  (1) June 17   *Silly Hoots*
  (2) Aug. 1   *Silly Hoots*
  (3) Sept. 12 *Silly Hoots*
  (4) Oct. 10   *Silly Hoots*
  (5) Nov. 7   *A Double Life*
  (6) Dec. 12   *Are You Married*

1921

  (7)   Jan. 9   *Silly Hoots*
  (8)   March 6   *Cabaret Courtesy*
  (9)   March 27 *Silly Hoots*
 (10) April 24 *Silly Hoots*

In *Paramount Cartoons*
 (11) May 22   *Padding the Bill*
 (12) June 19   *The Chicken Fancier*
 (13) July 24   *No Tickee No Shirtee*
 (14) Aug. 14 *Black Magic*

99. *Such Is Life*

Hy Mayer
Producer/Director/Story/Animation: Hy (Henry) Mayer
Distributor: Pathé Exchange
In *Pathé Review*

1920

  (1) Oct. 2   *Such Is Life Among the Dogs*
  (2) Oct. 16   *Such Is Life at the Zoo*
  (3) Nov. 6   *Such Is Life at Coney Island*
  (4) Nov. 13   *Such Is Sporting Life*
  (5) Nov. 20   *Such Is Life in Greenwich Village*
  (6) Dec. 4   *Such Is Life in Midwinter*
  (7) Dec. 18   *Such Is Life in East Side New York*

1921

  (8) Jan. 30   *Such Is Life in the Land of Fancy*

(9)   Feb. 19   *Such Is Life at a County Fair*
(10)   March 12   *Such Is Life in Summer*
(11)   April 10   *Such Is Life in Ramblerville*
(12)   July 3   *Such Is Life at the Race Track*
(13)   July 17   *Such Is Life at the Zoo*
(14)   Nov. 20   *Such Is Life in New York*

1922
(15)   Feb. 27   *Such Is Life*

Distributor: R.C. Pictures/Film Booking Offices

1922
(16)   April 15   *Such Is Life in London's West End*
(17)   May 7   *Such Is Life in Vollendam*
(18)   May 31   *Such Is Life in Monte Carlo*
(19)   June 4   *Such Is Life in Mon Petit Paris*
(20)   June 18   *Such Is Life Among the Children of France*
(21)   July 22   *Such Is Life in Munich*
(22)   July 22   *Such Is Life in Montmartre*
(23)   Aug. 12   *Such Is Life on the Riviera*
(24)   Aug. 12   *Such Is Life Among the Paris Shoppers*
(25)   Aug. 19   *Such Is Life Near London*
(26)   Aug. 27   *Such Is Life in Amsterdam and Alkmaar*
(27)   Oct.   *Such Is Life Among the Idlers of Paris*
(28)   Nov. 4   *Such Is Life in Busy London*
(29)   Nov.   *Such Is Life at a Dutch County Fair*
(30)   Dec.   *Such Is Life in Italy*

100.   Peanut Comedies

Producer/Director/Story/Animation: Harry D. Leonard
Camera: Harry E. Squires
Distributor: Paramount Pictures
Combination of live action and animation.
In *Paramount Magazine*

1920
(1)   Nov. 21   *One Hundred Per Cent Proof*

1921

  (2) Jan. 9   *Some Sayings of Benjamin Franklin*
  (3) March 20 *The Sheriff*
In *Paramount Cartoons*

1921

  (4) May 15   *Spaghetti for Two*
  (5) June 5   *In Old Madrid*
  (6) Aug. 8   *School Days*

101. *Paramount Cartoons*

Continuation of *Paramount Magazine.*
Distributor: Paramount Pictures

1921

  (1)   May 8   *Bobby Bumps Working on an Idea*
                  Director: Earl Hurd
  (2)   May 15 *Spaghetti for Two*
                  Director: Harry Leonard
  (3)   and   *Felix Goes on Strike*
                  Director: Pat Sullivan
  (4)   May 22 *Padding the Bill*
                  Director: Harry Bailey
  (5)   May 29 *By the Sea*
                  Director: Frank Moser
  (6)   June 5   *In Old Madrid*
                  Director: Harry Leonard
  (7)   and   *Felix in the Love Punch*
                  Director: Pat Sullivan
  (8)   June 12 *Shootin' Fish*
                  Director: Earl Hurd
  (9)   June 19 *The Chicken Fancier*
                  Director: Harry Bailey
 (10)   June 26 *$10,000 Under a Pillow*
                  Director: Frank Moser
 (11)   July 3   *Felix Out of Luck*
                  Director: Pat Sullivan
 (12)   July 9   *Bobby Bumps in Shadow Boxing*
                  Director: Earl Hurd

(13) July 17   *Felix Left at Home*
                Director: Pat Sullivan
(14) July 24   *No Tickee No Shirtee*
                Director: Harry Bailey
(15) July 31   *Dashing North*
                Director: Frank Moser
(16) Aug. 8   *School Days*
                Director: Harry Leonard
(17) Aug. 14   *Black Magic*
                Director: Harry Bailey
(18) Aug. 21   *Bobby Bumps in Hunting and Fishing*
                Director: Earl Hurd
(19) Aug. 28   *Kitchen Bedroom and Bath*
                Director: Frank Moser

102. *Aesop's Film Fables*

Fables Pictures, Inc.
Producer: Amedee J. Van Beuren
Directors: Paul Terry, John Foster, Hugh M. Shields, Frank Moser, Harry D. Bailey, Mannie Davis
Animation: Paul Terry, John C. Terry, John Foster, Hugh M. Shields, Frank Moser, Harry D. Bailey, Mannie Davis
Distributor: Pathé Exchange

1921

(1)   May 13   *The Goose That Laid the Golden Egg*
(2)   May 13   *Mice in Council*
(3)   May 13   *The Rooster and the Eagle*
(4)   May 13   *The Ants and the Grasshopper*
(5)   May 13   *Cats at Law*
(6)   May 13   *The Lioness and the Bugs*
(7)   May 13   *The Country Mouse and City Mouse*
(8)   May 13   *The Cat and the Canary*
(9)   May 13   *The Fox and Crow*
(10) May 13   *The Donkey in the Lion's Skin*
(11) May 13   *Mice at War*
(12) May 13   *The Hare and Frogs*
(13) May 13   *The Fashionable Fox*

(14)	May 13	*The Hermit and the Bear*
(15)	May 13	*The Hare and the Tortoise*
(16)	May 13	*The Wolf and the Crane*
(17)	May 13	*The Fox and the Goat*
(18)	Oct. 15	*Venus and the Cat*
(19)	Oct. 15	*The Frog and the Ox*
(20)	Oct. 15	*The Dog and the Bone*
(21)	Oct. 15	*The Cat and the Monkey*
(22)	Oct. 15	*The Owl and the Grasshopper*
(23)	Oct. 15	*The Woman and the Hen*
(24)	Oct. 15	*The Fly and the Ant*
(25)	Nov. 27	*The Frogs That Wanted a King*
(26)	Dec. 6	*The Conceited Donkey*
(27)	Dec. 6	*The Wolf and the Kid*
(28)	Dec. 10	*The Wayward Dog*
(29)	Dec. 31	*The Cat and the Mice*
(30)	Dec. 31	*The Dog and the Flea*

1922

(31)	Jan. 26	*The Bear and the Bees*
(32)	Jan. 26	*The Miller and His Donkey*
(33)	Jan. 26	*The Fox and the Grapes*
(34)	Jan. 26	*The Villain in Disguise*
(35)	Jan. 26	*The Dog and the Thief*
(36)	Jan. 26	*The Cat and the Swordfish*
(37)	Jan. 26	*The Tiger and the Donkey*
(38)	Jan. 26	*The Spendthrift*
(39)	Jan. 26	*The Farmer and the Ostrich*
(40)	Feb. 8	*The Dissatisfied Cobbler*
(41)	Feb. 21	*The Lion and the Mouse*
(42)	Feb. 21	*The Rich Cat and the Poor Cat*
(43)	March 4	*The Wolf in Sheep's Clothing*
(44)	March 4	*The Wicked Cat*
(45)	April 3	*The Boy and the Dog*
(46)	April 3	*The Eternal Triangle*
(47)	April 11	*The Model Dairy*
(48)	April 11	*Love at First Sight*
(49)	April 27	*The Hunter and His Dog*
(50)	April 27	*The Dog and the Wolves*

(51)	April 27	*The Maid and the Millionaire*
(52)	May 17	*The Farmer and His Cat*
(53)	May 17	*The Cat and the Pig*
(54)	May 29	*Crime in a Big City*
(55)	June 22	*Brewing Trouble*
(56)	June 22	*The Dog and the Fish*
(57)	June 22	*The Mischievous Cat*
(58)	June 22	*The Worm that Turned*
(59)	June 22	*The Boastful Cat*
(60)	June 26	*The Country Mouse and the City Cat*
(61)	June 26	*The Farmer and the Mice*
(62)	July 20	*Fearless Fido*
(63)	Aug. 9	*The Mechanical Horse*
(64)	Aug. 9	*The Boy and the Bear*
(65)	Aug. 12	*The Two Explorers*
(66)	Aug. 12	*The Two Slick Traders*
(67)	Sept. 27	*Two of a Trade*
(68)	Sept. 27	*The Big Flood*
(69)	Sept. 27	*The Romantic Mouse*
(70)	Sept. 27	*Henpecked Harry*
(71)	Sept. 27	*The Hated Rivals*
(72)	Sept. 27	*The Elephant's Trunk*
(73)	Sept. 27	*The Enchanted Fiddle*
(74)	Oct. 9	*The Rolling Stone*
(75)	Nov. 11	*Friday the Thirteenth*
(76)	Nov. 11	*The Fortune Hunters*
(77)	Nov. 11	*The Man Who Laughs*
(78)	Nov. 11	*Henry's Busted Romance*
(79)	Dec. 1	*The Two Trappers*
(80)	Dec. 1	*The Dog's Paradise*
(81)	Dec. 1	*The Frog and the Catfish*
(82)	Dec. 14	*Cheating the Cheaters*
(83)	Dec. 14	*A Stone Age Romeo*

1923

(84)	Jan. 27	*A Fisherman's Jinx*
(85)	Feb. 3	*A Raisin and a Cake of Yeast*
(86)	Feb. 10	*The Gliders*
(87)	Feb. 17	*Troubles on the Ark*

(88)	Feb. 17	*The Mysterious Hat*
(89)	Feb. 17	*The Traveling Salesman*
(90)	Feb. 17	*The Spider and the Fly*
(91)	Feb. 17	*The Sheik*
(92)	Feb. 17	*The Alley Cat*
(93)	Feb. 23	*Farmer Al Falfa's Bride*
(94)	March 22	*Day by Day in Every Way*
(95)	March 22	*One Hard Pull*
(96)	March 22	*The Gamblers*
(97)	March 22	*The Jolly Rounders*
(98)	April 27	*Pharaoh's Tomb*
(99)	April 27	*The Mouse Catcher*
(100)	April 27	*A Fishy Story*
(101)	April 27	*Spooks*
(102)	April 27	*Amateur Night on the Ark*
(103)	May 12	*The Stork's Mistake*
(104)	May 12	*Springtime*
(105)	June 6	*The Burglar Alarm*
(106)	June 6	*The Beauty Parlor*
(107)	June 6	*The Covered Pushcart*
(108)	June 7	*The Pace that Kills*
(109)	July 19	*Mysteries of the Sea*
(110)	July 19	*The Marathon Dancers*
(111)	July 19	*The Pearl Divers*
(112)	July 19	*The Bad Bandit*
(113)	July 19	*The Great Explorers*
(114)	Aug. 2	*The Nine of Spades*
(115)	Aug. 7	*The Cat That Failed*
(116)	Aug. 11	*The Walrus Hunters*
(117)	Aug. 11	*The Cat's Revenge*
(118)	Sept. 1	*Love in a Cottage*
(119)	Sept. 1	*Derby Day*
(120)	Sept. 1	*The Cat's Whiskers*
(121)	Sept. 29	*Aged in the Wood*
(122)	Sept. 29	*The High Flyers*
(123)	Sept. 29	*The Circus*
(124)	Sept. 29	*A Barnyard Rodeo*
(125)	Nov. 9	*Do Women Pay?*
(126)	Nov. 9	*Farmer Al Falfa's Pet Cat*

(127)	Nov. 9	*Happy Go Luckies*
(128)	Nov. 9	*The Five Fifteen*
(129)	Nov. 9	*The Best Man Wins*
(130)	Nov. 23	*A Dark Horse*
(131)	Nov. 16	*The Cat Came Back*
(132)	Nov. 16	*The Morning After*
(133)	Dec. 22	*Five Orphans of the Storm*
(134)	Dec. 24	*The Good Old Days*
(135)	Dec. 14	*The Animals' Fair*

1924

(136)	Jan. 9	*The Black Sheep*
(137)	Jan. 26	*Good Old College Days*
(138)	Jan. 26	*The Rat's Revenge*
(139)	Jan. 26	*A Rural Romance*
(140)	Feb. 20	*Captain Kidder*
(141)	Feb. 20	*Herman the Great Mouse*
(142)	Feb. 20	*The All Star Cast*
(143)	Feb. 20	*Why Mice Leave Home*
(144)	Feb. 20	*From Rags to Riches and Back Again*
(145)	March 20	*The Champion*
(146)	March 20	*Runnin' Wild*
(147)	April 22	*If Noah Lived Today*
(148)	April 22	*A Trip to the Pole*
(149)	April 22	*An Ideal Farm*
(150)	April 22	*Homeless Pups*
(151)	April 22	*When Winter Comes*
(152)	April 22	*The Jealous Fisherman*
(153)	May 12	*The Jolly Jailbird*
(154)	May 31	*One Good Turn Deserves Another*
(155)	May 28	*The Flying Carpet*
(156)	May 29	*The Organ Grinder*
(157)	June 14	*That Old Can of Mine*
(158)	June 28	*Home Talent*
(159)	July 5	*The Body in the Bag*
(160)	July 12	*Desert Sheiks*
(161)	July 19	*A Woman's Honor*
(162)	July 26	*The Sport of Kings*
(163)	Aug. 2	*Flying Fever*

(164)	Aug. 2	*Amelia Comes Back*
(165)	Aug. 2	*The Prodigal Pup*
(166)	Aug. 2	*House Cleaning*
(167)	Sept. 5	*The Barnyard Olympics*
(168)	Sept. 5	*A Message from the Sea*
(169)	Sept. 13	*In the Good Old Summer Time*
(170)	Sept. 20	*The Mouse That Turned*
(171)	Sept. 25	*A Lighthouse by the Sea*
(172)	Sept. 25	*Hawks of the Sea*
(173)	Sept. 25	*Noah's Outing*
(174)	Oct. 18	*Black Magic*
(175)	Oct. 29	*The Cat and the Magnet*
(176)	Oct. 29	*Monkey Business*
(177)	Oct. 29	*She Knew Her Man*
(178)	Nov. 22	*Good Old Circus Days*
(179)	Nov. 22	*Lumber Jacks*
(180)	Dec. 3	*Noah's Athletic Club*
(181)	Dec. 3	*Mysteries of Old Chinatown*
(182)	Dec. 3	*Down on the Farm*
(183)	Dec. 3	*On the Ice*
(184)	Dec. 3	*Sharp Shooters*
(185)	Dec. 3	*She's in Again*
(186)	Dec. 11	*One Game Pup*
(187)	Dec. 11	*African Huntsmen*
(188)	Dec. 26	*Hold That Thought*
(189)	Dec. 31	*Biting the Dust*

1925

(190)	Jan. 19	*A Transatlantic Flight*
(191)	Jan. 19	*Bigger and Better Jails*
(192)	Jan. 19	*Fisherman's Luck*
(193)	Feb. 9	*Clean Up Week*
(194)	Feb. 13	*In Dutch*
(195)	Feb. 13	*Jungle Bike Riders*
(196)	Feb. 13	*The Pie Man*
(197)	March 5	*At the Zoo*
(198)	March 26	*The Housing Shortage*
(199)	March 26	*S.O.S.*
(200)	April 10	*The Adventures of Adenoid*

(201)	April 10	*Permanent Waves*
(202)	April 25	*Deep Stuff*
(203)	May 4	*House Cleaning*
(204)	May 4	*Darkest Africa*
(205)	May 4	*A Fast Worker*
(206)	May 4	*Echoes from the Alps*
(207)	May 4	*Hot Times in Iceland*
(208)	May 4	*The Runt*
(209)	May 8	*The End of the World*
(210)	May 8	*The Runaway Balloon*
(211)	May 18	*Wine, Women and Song*
(212)	May 18	*When Men Were Men*
(213)	June 11	*Bugville Field Day*
(214)	June 11	*Office Help*
(215)	June 23	*Over the Plate*
(216)	July 6	*A Yarn about a Yarn*
(217)	July 6	*Bubbles*
(218)	July 6	*Soap*
(219)	July 20	*For the Love of a Gal*
(220)	July 20	*Window Washers*
(221)	July 20	*Barnyard Follies*
(222)	Aug. 28	*The Ugly Duckling*
(223)	Aug. 28	*Hungry Hounds*
(224)	Aug. 28	*Nuts and Squirrels*
(225)	Aug. 28	*The Lion and the Monkey*
(226)	Sept. 28	*The Hero Wins*
(227)	Sept. 28	*Air Cooled*
(228)	Sept. 28	*Closer than a Brother*
(229)	Sept. 28	*Wild Cats of Paris*
(230)	Sept. 28	*The Honor System*
(231)	Nov. 6	*The Great Open Spaces*
(232)	Nov. 21	*More Mice than Brains*
(233)	Nov. 28	*A Day's Outing*
(234)	Dec. 5	*The Bonehead Age*
(235)	Dec. 12	*The Haunted House*
(236)	Dec. 17	*The English Channel Swim*
(237)	Dec. 17	*Noah Had His Troubles*
		aka: Noah and His Trousers

1926

(238)	Jan. 23	*The Gold Push*
(239)	Jan. 23	*Three Blind Mice*
(240)	Jan. 23	*Lighter than Air*
(241)	Jan. 23	*Little Brown Jug*
(242)	Jan. 23	*The June Bride*
(243)	Jan. 23	*The Wind Jammers*
(244)	Jan. 23	*The Wicked City*
(245)	Jan. 23	*Hunting in 1950*
(246)	Feb. 6	*The Mail Coach*
(247)	Feb. 6	*Spanish Love*
(248)	March 6	*The Fire Fighters*
(249)	March 6	*Up in the Air*
(250)	March 6	*Fly Time*
(251)	March 12	*The Merry Blacksmith*
(252)	April 20	*The Big-hearted Fish*
(253)	April 20	*The Shootin' Fool*
(254)	April 20	*The Farm Hands*
(255)	April 20	*Rough and Ready Romeo*
(256)	May 17	*An Alpine Flapper*
(257)	May 17	*Liquid Dynamite*
(258)	May 26	*A Bumper Crop*
(259)	May 26	*The Big Retreat*
(260)	July 6	*The Land Boom*
(261)	July 6	*A Plumber's Life*
(262)	July 6	*Chop Suey and Noodles*
(263)	July 6	*Jungle Sports*
(264)	July 8	*Red Hot Sands*
(265)	July 22	*Pirates Bold*
(266)	July 22	*Venus of Venice*
(267)	July 22	*Her Ben*
(268)	July 22	*Dough Boys*
(269)	July 26	*The Little Parade*
(270)	July 26	*The Last Ha-Ha*
(271)	Aug. 22	*Scrambled Eggs*
(272)	Aug. 28	*A Knight Out*
(273)	Sept. 11	*A Buggy Ride*
(274)	Sept. 17	*Pests*
(275)	Sept. 17	*Watered Stock*

(276)	Sept. 17	*The Charleston Queen*
(277)	Sept. 17	*Why Argue*
(278)	Sept. 29	*The Road House*
(279)	Oct. 22	*Gun Shy*
(280)	Oct. 26	*Home Sweet Home*
(281)	Oct. 22	*The Phoney Express*
(282)	Oct. 26	*Thru Thick and Thin*
(283)	Oct. 26	*In Vaudeville*
(284)	Oct. 26	*Buck Fever*
(285)	Oct. 26	*Radio Controlled*
(286)	Oct. 26	*Hitting the Rails*
(287)	Dec. 6	*Sink or Swim*
(288)	Dec. 31	*Bars and Stripes*
(289)	Dec. 31	*School Days*
(290)	Dec. 31	*The Musical Parrot*
(291)	Dec. 31	*Where Friendship Ceases*

1927

(292)	Jan. 13	*The Plowboy's Revenge*
(293)	Jan. 13	*Chasing Rainbows*
(294)	Jan. 22	*In the Rough*
(295)	Jan. 22	*Tit for Tat*
(296)	Feb. 14	*The Mail Pilot*
(297)	Feb. 19	*Cracked Ice*
(298)	March 4	*Taking the Air*
(299)	March 4	*All for a Bride*
(300)	March 12	*The Magician*
(301)	March 12	*The Crawl Stroke Kid*
(302)	April 1	*The Medicine Man*
(303)	April 1	*Keep Off the Grass*
(304)	April 1	*Anti-Fat*
(305)	April 1	*The Honor Man*
(306)	May 6	*The Pie-Eyed Piper*
(307)	May 6	*Bubbling Over*
(308)	May 6	*A Fair Exchange*
(309)	May 6	*When the Snow Flies*
(310)	May 12	*A Dog's Day*
(311)	May 12	*Horse, Horses, Horses*
(312)	May 12	*Hard Cider*

(313)	May 12	*Digging for Gold*
(314)	May 12	*Died in the Wool*
(315)	May 12	*A One-Man Dog*
(316)	May 12	*The Big Reward*
(317)	May 12	*Riding High*
(318)	June 7	*The Love Nest*
(319)	June 20	*The Bully*
(320)	June 20	*Subway Sally*
(321)	June 20	*Ant Life as It Isn't*
(322)	June 26	*The Baby Show*
(323)	July 6	*Jungle Sports*
(324)	July 8	*Red Hot Sands*
(325)	July 8	*A Hole in One*
(326)	July 22	*Hook, Line and Sinker*
(327)	July 22	*A Small Town Sheriff*
(328)	July 22	*Cutting a Melon*
(329)	Aug. 16	*The Human Fly*
(330)	Aug. 16	*The River of Doubt*
(331)	Aug. 16	*In Again, Out Again*
(332)	Aug. 16	*All Bull and a Yard Wide*
(333)	Sept. 2	*The Big Tent*
(334)	Sept. 2	*Lindy's Cat*
(335)	Sept. 17	*A Brave Heart*
(336)	Sept. 29	*Signs of Spring*
(337)	Oct. 13	*The Fox Hunt*
(338)	Oct. 26	*Flying Fishers*
(339)	Nov. 19	*Carnival Week*
		Director: John Foster
(340)	Nov. 19	*Rats in His Garret*
		Director: Hugh Shields
(341)	Nov. 28	*The Junk Man*
		Director: Mannie Davis
(342)	Dec. 12	*High Stakes*
		Director: Hugh Shields
(343)	Dec.	*The Home Agent*
(344)	Dec.	*A Horse's Tale*

1928

(345)	Jan. 4	*The Wandering Minstrel*

Director: Harry Bailey
(346) Jan. 6 *The Good Ship Nellie*
Director: Frank Moser
(347) Jan. 17 *Everybody's Flying*
Director: John Foster
(348) Jan. 24 *The Spider's Lair*
Director: Mannie Davis
(349) Jan. 28 *A Blaze of Glory*
Director: Mannie Davis
(350) Jan. 28 *The County Fair*
(351) Feb. 8 *On the Ice*
Director: Frank Moser
(352) Feb. *The Sea Shower*
(353) March 19 *Jungle Days*
Director: John Foster
(354) March 21 *Scaling the Alps*
Director: Mannie Davis
(355) April 2 *Barnyard Lodge Number One*
Director: Frank Moser
(356) April 2 *A Battling Duet*
(357) April 8 *Barnyard Artists*
Director: Hugh Shields
(358) April 14 *A Jungle Triangle*
Director: Mannie Davis
(359) April 18 *Coast to Coast*
Director: Frank Moser
(360) April 20 *The War Bride*
Director: Harry Bailey
(361) April 30 *The Flying Age*
Director: John Foster
(362) May 7 *The Flight That Failed*
Director: Hugh Shields
(363) May 9 *Happy Days*
(364) May 10 *Puppy Love*
Director: Mannie Davis
(365) June 12 *City Slickers*
Director: Harry Bailey
(366) June 26 *The Huntsman*
Director: Frank Moser

(367) June 26 *The Baby Show*
                Director: Mannie Davis
(368) June 26 *The Early Bird*
                Director: John Foster
(369) July 2   *Our Little Nell*
                Director: Frank Moser
(370) July 9   *Outnumbered*
                Director: Hugh Shields
(371) July 26 *Sunny Italy*
                Director: Mannie Davis
(372) July 26 *A Cross Country Run*
                Director: Harry Bailey
(373) Aug. 14 *Static*
(374) Aug. 16 *Sunday on the Farm*
                Director: John Foster
(375) Aug. 16 *Alaska or Bust*
                Director: Frank Moser
(376) Sept. 10 *High Seas*
                Director: Mannie Davis
(377) Sept. 17 *The Magnetic Bat*
(378) Sept. 20 *Kill or Cure*
                Director: Hugh Shields
(379) Sept. 24 *Monkey Love*
                Director: Mannie Davis
(380) Oct. 2   *The Big Game*
                Director: Harry Bailey
(381) Oct. 4   *Grid Iron Demons*
                Director: Frank Moser
(382) Oct. 26 *The Laundry Man*
(383) Nov. 10 *On the Links*
(384) Nov. 24 *A Day Off*
                Director: John Foster
(385) Nov. 26 *Barnyard Politics*
                Director: Hugh Shields
(386) Dec. 3   *Flying Hoofs*
                Director: Harry Bailey
(387) Dec. 17 *Dinner Time*
                Director: John Foster

(NB: First *Aesop's Fables* cartoon with sound;
also released silent.)

(388) Dec. 27 *A White Elephant*
                Director: Hugh Shields
(389) Dec. 28 *Land o' Cotton*
                Director: Frank Moser

1929
(390) Jan. 2   *Break of Day*
                Director: Mannie Davis
(391) Jan. 6   *Snapping the Whip*
                Director: Harry Bailey
(392) Jan. 6   *Wooden Money*
                Director: John Foster
(393) Jan. 8   *Sweet Adeline*
                Director: Frank Moser
(394) Jan. 30 *The Queen Bee*
                Director: Hugh Shields
(395) Feb. 11 *Grandma's House*
(396) Feb. 12 *Back to the Soil*
(397) March 1 *The Black Duck*
(398) March 2 *A Lad and His Lamp*
(399) March 11 *The Big Burg*
(400) March 13 *The Under Dog*
(401) March 17 *The Cop's Bride*
(402) April 12 *The Big Shot*
(403) April 26 *The Fight Game*
(404) April 26 *Homeless Cats*
(405) April 29 *The Little Game Hunter*
(406) May 4   *The Ball Park*
(407) May 4   *Concentrate*
(408) May 4   *The Faithful Pup*
(409) May 6   *The Jail Breakers*
(410) May 8   *Fish Day*
(411) May 9   *Custard Pies*
(412) May 9   *The Wood Choppers*
(413) May 20   *Presto Change-o*
(414) May 20   *The Polo Match*
(415) May 24   *Snow Birds*

(416)	May 27	*Skating Hounds*
(417)	June 2	*Kidnapped*
(418)	June 14	*April Showers*
(419)	June 19	*The Farmer's Goat*

Director: John Foster

(420)	June 23	*Cold Steel*
(421)	June 25	*In His Cups*
(422)	July 8	*By Land and Air*

Director: John Foster

(423)	July 29	*The Enchanted Flute*

Director: Frank Moser

(424)	July 29	*Wash Day*

Director: Mannie Davis

(425)	Aug. 14	*Cabaret*

Director: Frank Moser

(426)	Aug. 15	*The Big Scare*
(427)	Aug. 22	*Fruitful Farm*

Director: John Foster

(NB: Last silent *Aesop's Fables* cartoon. Series becomes *Aesop's Sound Film Fables*.)

103. *Tony Sarg's Almanac*

Dawley
Producer/Camera: Herbert M. Dawley
Story/Animation: Tony Sarg, Herbert M. Dawley
Distributor: Rialto Productions
"Shadowgraphs": animated marionettes in silhouette.

1921

(1)	May 21	*The First Circus*
(2)	June	*The First Dentist*
(3)	July 2	*Why They Love Cave Men*
(4)	Aug. 20	*When the Whale Was Jonahed*
(5)	Sept. 10	*Fireman Save My Child*

1922

(6)	Jan. 7	*The Original Golfer*
(7)	Feb. 5	*Why Adam Walked the Floor* (740)
(8)	April 9	*The Original Movie* (772)

(9) May 29   *The First Earful*
(10) July 9   *Noah Put the Cat Out*

Distributor: Educational Pictures

1922
(11) July 29   *The First Flivver*
(12) July 29   *The First Degree*
(13) Aug. 19   *The First Barber*
(14) Sept. 9   *Baron Bragg and the Devilish Dragon*
(15) Nov. 19   *The Ogling Ogre*
(16) Dec. 17   *Baron Bragg and the Haunted Castle*

1923
(17) Jan. 6   *The Terrible Tree*

104. *MacDono Cartoons*

MacDono Cartoons Inc.
Producers/Directors/Story/Animation: J.J. McManus, R.E.
  Donahue
Distributor: Affiliated Distributors

1921
(1) June 4   *Mr. Ima Jonah's Home Brew*
(2) June 4   *Skipping the Pen*

Distributor: Mastodon Films

1922
(3) March 1   *Burr's Novelty Review No. 1*
(4) April 1   *Burr's Novelty Review No. 2*
(5) May 1   *Burr's Novelty Review No. 3*
(6) June 1   *Burr's Novelty Review No. 4*
(7) July 1   *Burr's Novelty Review No. 5*
(8) Aug. 1   *Burr's Novelty Review No. 6*

105. *Sketchografs*

aka: Sketchographs

Ollendorff
Producer/Director/Story/Animation: Julian Ollendorff
Distributor: Educational Pictures

1921

(1)	Aug. 7	*Play Ball*
(2)	Sept. 16	*Just for Fun*
(3)	Oct.	*Eve's Leaves*
(4)	Nov.	*Seeing Greenwich Village*
(5)	Dec. 24	*What's the Limit*

Distributor: Pathé

1921

(6)	Sept. 18	*Jiggin' on the Old Sod* in *Pathé Review No. 121*

In *The Graphic*
Animated sequences included in weekly magazine film series.
Distributor: Educational Pictures

1922

(7)	Oct. 21	*Famous Men*
(8)	Oct. 28	*Athletics and Women*
(9)	Nov. 4	*Champions*
(10)	Nov. 11	*Animals and Humans*
(11)	Dec. 2	*Mackerel Fishing*
(12)	Dec. 16	*The Coastguard*

1923

Series of 12 films; only the first title traced:

(13)	Jan. 8	*Family Album*

1926

Distributor: Cranfield and Clarke

(14)	Sept. 1	*Beauty and the Beach*
(15)	Sept. 15	*Everybody Rides*
(16)	Oct. 1	*Fair Weather*
(17)	Oct. 15	*The Big Show*
(18)	Nov. 1	*Watch Your Step*
(19)	Nov. 15	*Revolution of the Sexes*

(20) Dec. 1   *Tin Pan Alley*
(NB: 5 further films, titles untraced)

106. *Dreams of a Rarebit Fiend*

GB: *Rarebit Cartoons*
Rialto Productions
Producer / Director / Story: Winsor McCay
Animation: Winsor McCay, Robert McCay, John A. Fitzsimmons
Based on the comic strip by Winsor McCay.

1921
(1) Sept. 26   *Bug Vaudeville*
(2) Sept. 26   *The Pet*
               GB: *The Last Word*
(3) Sept. 26   *The Flying House*
               GB: *Watch Your House*
(4)   *The Centaurs*
(5)   *Flip's Circus*
(6)   *Gertie on Tour*

107. *The American Picture Book*

Aywon Film Corporation

1922
(1) March 11   *The American Picture Book*
("A series of decidedly novel animated
drawings.")

108. *Laugh-O-Grams*

Laugh-O-Gram Films
Producer / Director: Walter E. Disney
Screenplay: Walter J. Pfeiffer
Animation: Ubbe Iwerks, Hugh Harman, Rudolf Ising, Carman
Maxwell, Lorey Tague, Otto Walliman
Camera: W. "Red" Lyon
Distributor: Leslie B. Mace

1922

(1)	July 29	*Little Red Riding Hood*
(2)	Aug.	*The Four Musicians of Bremen*
(3)	Sept.	*Jack and the Beanstalk*
(4)	Oct.	*Goldilocks and the Three Bears*
(5)	Nov.	*Puss in Boots*
(6)	Dec.	*Cinderella*
(7)	Dec.	*Tommy Tucker's Tooth*

109. *Earl Hurd Comedies*

Earl Hurd Productions
Producer/Director/Story/Animation: Earl Hurd
Distributor: Educational Pictures
Combined animation and live action.

1922

(1)	Aug. 5	*One Ol' Cat*
		Distributor: Mastodon Cartoons
(2)	Aug. 26	*Fresh Fish*
(3)	Dec. 2	*Railroading*

1923

(4)	Feb. 18	*The Message of Emile Coué*
(5)	Feb. 24	*Chicken Dressing*
(6)	April 1	*The Movie Daredevil*
(7)	June 2	*Their Love Growed Cold*

110. *Roving Thomas*

aka: *The Adventures of Roving Thomas*
aka: *Cat Cartoons*
Kineto Films
Producer: Charles Urban
Distributor: Vitagraph
Live action and animation combined.

1922

(1)	Sept. 17	*Roving Thomas Sees New York*

(2) Oct. 22 *Roving Thomas on an Aeroplane*
(3) Dec. 10 *Roving Thomas on a Fishing Trip*

1923
(4) Feb. *Roving Thomas at the Winter Carnival*
(5) April *Roving Thomas*
(6) June *Roving Thomas*
(7) Aug. *Roving Thomas*
(8) Oct. 27 *Roving Thomas in Chicago*
(NB: Reissued in 1927 by Film Exchange Inc.)

111. Hodge Podge

aka: *Lyman H. Howe's Hodge Podge*
Lyman H. Howe Films Company
Producer: Lyman H. Howe
Supervisor: Robert Gillsum
Screenplays: James F. Clemenger
Animation: Leslie Elton, Archie N. Griffith, Whitfield War-
   mouth
Distributor: Educational Films Corporation
Animated sequences included in live-action magazine films.

1922
(1) Oct. 8 *King Winter*
          Some Sense and Nonsense
(2) Nov. 1 *Sea Elephants*
          Burlesque Newsreel
(3) Dec. 8 *The Garden of Geysers*

1923
(4) Jan. 23 *Hot Shots*
          Old King Cole
(5) Jan. 6 *Mrs. Hippo*
(6) March 14 *Fishing for Tarpon*
          A Tragedy in Dogville
(7) May 2 *Speed Demons*
(8) May 17 *Shooting the Earth*
(9) July 18 *A Flivver Elopement*

(10) July 18 *The Cat and the Fiddle*
(11) Aug. 11 *Dipping in the Deep*
The Stag Hunt
(12) Sept. 29 *Why the Globe Trotter Trots*
(13) Oct. 16 *Speedville*
People of Many Climes
(14) Nov. 19 *The Bottom of the Sea*
(15) Dec. 17 *Liquid Love*

1924
(16) Jan. 16 *A Sailor's Life*
(17) Feb. 9 *Movie Pioneer*
(18) March 13 *Jumping Jacks*
(19) April 19 *The Realm of Sport*
Santa Claus
(20) May 1 *A Tiny Tour of the U.S.A.*
(21) June 12 *Snapshots of the Universe*
(22) July 26 *Frozen Water*
(23) Aug. 29 *Hazardous Hunting*
Radio Station J.U.N.K.
(24) Sept. 18 *A Crazy Quilt of Travel*
(25) Oct. 16 *Whirligigs*
(26) Nov. 28 *Earth's Oddities*
(27) Dec. 28 *Hi-Flyers*

1925
(28) Jan. 25 *Topsy Turvy Travel*
(29) Feb. 16 *Lots of Knots*
(30) March 27 *Movie Morsels*
(31) April 19 *The Village School*
(32) May 26 *Earth's Other Half*
Swiss Cheese
(33) June 16 *Mexican Melody*
(34) June 30 *Travel Treasures*
(35) Aug. 1 *Pictorial Proverbs*
(36) Aug. 22 *The Story Teller*
(37) Oct. 18 *Knicknacks of Knowledge*
(38) Nov. 16 *Magical Movies*
(39) Dec. 21 *A Mythical Monster*

1926

(40)	Jan. 20	*Mother Goose's Movies*
(41)	Feb. 16	*Criss Cross Cruise*
(42)	March 20	*Congress of Celebrities*
(43)	April 12	*Neptune's Domain*
(44)	May 23	*From A to Z thru Filmdom*
(45)	June 22	*Peeking at the Planets*
(46)	July 25	*Chips of the Old Block*
(47)	Aug. 22	*Alligator's Paradise*
(48)	Sept. 19	*A Merrygoround of Travel*
(49)	Oct. 26	*Figures of Fancy*
(50)	Nov. 28	*A Keyhole Cruise*
(51)	Dec. 26	*Movie Medley*

1927

(52)	Jan. 16	*A Cluster of Kings*
(53)	Feb. 13	*The Wise Old Owl*
(54)	March 13	*Climbing into Cloudland*
(55)	April 17	*A Bird of Flight*
(56)	May 22	*A Scenic Treasure Chest*
(57)	June 16	*Tales of a Traveler*
(58)	July 17	*Capers of a Camera*
(59)	Aug. 8	*Bubbles of Geography*
(60)	Aug. 30	*Delving into the Dictionary*
(61)	Oct. 16	*Here and There in Travel Land*
(62)	Nov. 13	*Models in Mud*
(63)	Dec. 11	*A Whirl of Activity*

1928

(64)	Jan. 8	*Recollections of a Rover*
(65)	Jan. 28	*Star Shots*
(66)	March 31	*How to Please the Public*
(67)	April 8	*Nicknames*
(68)	May 19	*The Wandering Toy*
(69)	June 19	*Pictorial Tidbits*
(70)	July 3	*Conquering the Colorado*
(71)	Aug. 7	*The Peep Show*
(72)	Sept. 28	*On the Move*
(73)	Nov. 2	*Glorious Adventure*
(74)	Nov. 30	*A Patchwork of Pictures*

1929
- (75) Jan. 11   *Shifting Scenes*
- (76) Jan. 25   *Question Marks*
- (77) March 15 *A Dominion of Diversity*
              (NB: Last issue of *Hodge Podge* as a silent
              series. Continued in sound.)

112. Technical Romances

Bray Productions
Producer: John R. Bray
Director/Story/Animation: J.A. Norling, Ashley Miller, F. Lyle
  Goldman
Distributor: Hodkinson

1922
- (1) Nov. 25 *The Mystery Box*
- (2) Dec. 9   *The Sky Splitter*

1923
- (3) Feb. 4   *Gambling with the Gulf Stream*
- (4) March 1 *The Romance of Life*
- (5) June 10 *The Immortal Voice*
- (6) Dec. 1   *Black Sunlight*

113. Ink-Ravings

Bray Productions
Producer: John R. Bray
Director/Story/Animation: Milt Gross
In *Bray Magazine*

1922
- (1) Dec. 16 *Scrap Hangers*
- (2) Dec. 30 *Taxes*

1923
- (3) Jan.   *If We Reversed*

114. *Silliettes*

Herbert M. Dawley
Producer/Director/Animation: Herbert M. Dawley
Distributor: Pathé Exchange
Animated silhouette sequences included in the magazine series
Pathé Review.

1923

(1)	March 24	*Silliettes*
(2)	April 7	*The Lobster Nightmare*
(3)	June 9	*The Absent Minded Poet*
(4)	July 7	*The Classic Centaur*

1924

(5)	Feb. 9	*Pan the Piper*
(6)	Sept. 27	*Thumbelina*
(7)		*Jack and the Beanstalk*
(8)		*Cinderella*
(9)		*Sleeping Beauty*
(10)		*Beauty and the Beast*
(11)		*Tattercoats*
(12)		*Aladdin and the Wonderful Lamp*

1925

(13)	May 9	*Jack the Giant Killer*

115. *Fun from the Press*

Out of the Inkwell Films
Producer: Max Fleischer
Director: Dave Fleischer
Animators: Dick Huemer, Roland Crandall, Burton Gillett
Distributor: Hodkinson
Series of animated sequences adapted from *The Literary Digest*
for inclusion in three magazine films.

1923

(1)	April 28	No. 1
(2)	May	No. 2
(3)	June	No. 3

116. Tom and Jerry

Arrow Film Corporation

1923
(1)	Aug. 1	*The Gasoline Trail*
(2)	Sept. 1	*Tom's First Flivver*

117. Red Head Comedies

Lee-Bradford Corporation
Producer/Director/Story/Animation: Frank A. Nankivell, W.E. Stark, "Hutch," Richard M. Friel
Series of cartoons in color.

1923
(1)	Sept.	*Robinson Crusoe Returns on Friday*
(2)	Sept.	*Cleopatra and Her Easy Mark*
(3)	Sept.	*Napoleon Not So Great*
(4)	Sept.	*Kidding Captain Kidd*
(5)	Sept.	*Rip Without a Wink*
(6)	Sept.	*Columbus Discovers a New Whirl*
(7)	Dec.	*Why Sitting Bull Stood Up*
(8)	Dec.	*What Did William Tell*
(9)	Dec.	*A Whale of a Story*
(10)	Dec.	*How Troy Was Collared*
(11)	Dec.	*The Jones Boys' Sister*

118. Alice Comedies

aka: *Alice in Cartoonland*
Walt Disney Comics
Producers: Walter E. Disney, Roy Disney
Directors: Walter E. Disney, Ubbe Iwerks
Animators: Ubbe Iwerks, Rollin Hamilton, Walker Harman, Hugh Harman, Rudolf Ising
Distributor: Winkler Pictures (Margaret J. Winkler)
Combined live action and animation: Alice played by Virginia Davis, Margie Gay, Dawn O'Day.

Reissued with synchronized sound by Syndicate Pictures (1929–1930).

1923

(1)   *Alice's Wonderland*

1924

(2) March 1 *Alice's Wild West Show*
(3) April 1 *Alice's Spooky Adventure*
(4) May 1 *Alice's Day at the Sea*
(5) June 1 *Alice's Fishy Story*
(6) July 1 *Alice and the Dog Catcher*
(7) Aug. 1 *Alice the Peacemaker*
(8) Oct. 15 *Alice Hunting in Africa*
(9) Nov. 1 *Alice Gets in Dutch*
(10) Dec. 1 *Alice and the Three Bears*
(11) Dec. 15 *Alice Plays the Piper*

1925

(12) Jan. 1 *Alice Cans the Cannibals*
(13) Jan. 15 *Alice the Toreador*
(14) Feb. 1 *Alice Gets Stung*
         (sound reissue: 10.15.29)
(15) Feb. 15 *Alice Solves the Puzzle*
         (sound reissue: 4.15.30)
(16) April 3 *Alice's Eggplant*
         (sound reissue: 12.1.29)
(17) April 29 *Alice Loses Out*
         (sound reissue: 3.1.30)
(18) May 5 *Alice Wins the Derby*
         (sound reissue: 11.15.29)
(19) Sept. 15 *Alice the Jail Bird*
         (sound reissue: 11.1.29)
(20) Oct. 1 *Alice Is Stage Struck*
         (sound reissue: 1.15.30)
(21) Oct. 15 *Alice Plays Cupid*
         (sound reissue: 4.1.30)
(22) Nov. 1 *Alice Picks the Champ*
         (sound reissue: 3.15.30)
(23) Nov. 15 *Alice's Tin Pony*
         (sound reissue: 9.15.29)

(24)	Dec. 1	*Alice Chops the Suey*
		(sound reissue: 2.1.30)
(25)	Dec. 15	*Alice in the Jungle*
		(sound reissue: 1.1.30)

1926

(26)	Jan. 1	*Alice on the Farm*
		(sound reissue: 10.1.29)
(27)	Jan. 15	*Alice Rattled by Rats*
		(sound reissue: 5.1.30)
(28)	Feb. 1	*Alice's Little Parade*
		(sound reissue: 9.1.29)
(29)	Feb. 15	*Alice's Mysterious Mystery*
		(sound reissue: 5.15.30)
(30)	March 1	*Alice's Balloon Race*
		(sound reissue: 12.15.29)
(31)	May 1	*Alice's Ornery Orphan*
		(sound reissue: 2.15.30)
(32)	June 28	*Alice Charms the Fish*
(33)	Sept. 18	*Alice's Monkey Business*
(34)	Sept. 29	*Alice in Slumberland*
(35)	Oct. 4	*Alice in the Wooly West*
(36)	Oct. 18	*Alice the Fire Fighter*
(37)	Nov. 1	*Alice Cuts the Ice*
(38)	Nov. 15	*Alice Helps the Romance*
(39)	Nov. 29	*Alice's Spanish Guitar*
(40)	Dec. 13	*Alice's Brown Derby*
(41)	Dec. 27	*Alice the Lumberjack*

1927

(42)	Jan. 10	*Alice the Golf Bug*
(43)	Jan. 24	*Alice Foils the Pirates*
(44)	Feb. 7	*Alice at the Carnival*
(45)	Feb. 21	*Alice at the Rodeo*
(46)	March 7	*Alice the Collegiate*
(47)	March 21	*Alice in the Alps*
(48)	April 4	*Alice's Auto Race*
(49)	April 18	*Alice's Circus Daze*
(50)	May 2	*Alice's Knaughty Knight*
(51)	May 15	*Alice's Three Bad Eggs*

(52) May 30   *Alice's Picnic*
(53) June 13   *Alice's Channel Swim*
(54) June 27   *Alice in the Klondike*
(55) July 11   *Alice's Medicine Show*
(56) July 25   *Alice the Whaler*
(57) Aug. 8   *Alice the Beach Nut*
(58) Aug. 22   *Alice in the Big League*

119. *Song Car-Tunes*

Out of the Inkwell Inc.
Producers: Max Fleischer, Alfred Weiss
Director: Dave Fleischer
Animation: Dave Fleischer, Dick Huemer, Roland Crandall,
   Burton Gillett, Art Davis
Camera: Charles Schettler
Distributor: Arrow Film Corp.

1924

(1) March 9   *Series A*
              "Mother Pin a Rose on Me," "Come Take a
              Trip in My Airship," "Goodbye My Lady
              Love"
(2) Sept. 15 *Series B*
              (song titles not traced)

Distributor: Red Seal Pictures Corp.

1925

(3) Jan. 15   *Come Take a Trip in My Airship*
(4) Feb. 1   *The Old Folks at Home*
(5) March 1   *Mother, Mother Pin a Rose on Me*
(6) March 20 *I Love a Lassie*
(7) April 25 *The Suwanee River*
(8) May 30   *Daisy Bell*
(9) Sept. 15 *My Bonnie Lies Over the Ocean*
               (NB: First "bouncing ball" cartoon)
(10) Oct. 15   *Ta-Ra-Ra-Boom-De-A*
(11) Nov. 15   *Dixie*
(12) Dec. 15   *Sailing, Sailing*

1926

(13) Feb. 6 *Dolly Gray*
(14) Feb. 21 *Has Anybody Here Seen Kelly*
(15) March 13 *My Old Kentucky Home*
(16) May 1 *Sweet Adeline*
(17) May 8 *Tramp Tramp Tramp*
(18) May 22 *Goodbye My Lady Love*
(19) June 1 *Coming Through the Rye*
(20) July 17 *Pack Up Your Troubles*
(21) July 17 *The Trail of the Lonesome Pine*
(22) Aug. 21 *By the Light of the Silvery Moon*
(23) Sept. *In the Good Old Summer Time*
(24) Sept. *Oh You Beautiful Doll*
(25) Nov. 1 *Old Black Joe*

1927

(26) April 1 *Jingle Bells*
(27) April 15 *Waiting for the Robert E. Lee*

120. Historiets

Reel Colors Inc.
Animated cartoons in color.

1924

(1) May *The Teapot Dome*
(2) May *Famous Sayings of Famous Americans*
(3) May *Witty Sayings of Witty Frenchmen*
(4) May *Witty Naughty Thoughts*

121. Pathé Review

Pathé Exchange
Cartoon item in weekly magazine film.

1920

(1) Oct. 2 *Such Is Life Among the Dogs*
          Hy Mayer
(2) Oct. 16 *The Zoo*
          Hy Mayer

(3) Oct. 6   *Coney Island*
                Hy Mayer
(4) Nov. 13   *Baseball*
                Hy Mayer
(5) Nov. 20   *Greenwich Village*
                Hy Mayer
(6) Dec. 4   *Winter Sports*
                Hy Mayer
(7) Dec. 18   *East Side New York*
                Hy Mayer

1921

(8) Jan. 15   *The Circus*
                Hy Mayer
(9) Feb. 5   *Travelaugh*
                Hy Mayer
(10) Feb. 19   *The County Fair*
                Hy Mayer
(11) March 12   *Water Stuff*
                Hy Mayer
(12) April 9   *Spring Hats*
                Hy Mayer
(13) April 30   *All the Merry Bow-Wows*
                Hy Mayer
(14) May 29   *In the Silly Summertime*
                Hy Mayer
(15) June 26   *The Door That Has No Lock*
                Hy Mayer
(16) July 3   *The Race Track*
                Hy Mayer
(17) July 17   *Scenes in the Zoo*
                Hy Mayer
(18) Aug.   *A Ramble Through Provincetown*
                Hy Mayer
(19) Sept. 4   *The Little City of Dreams*
                Hy Mayer
(20) Sept. 18   *Day Dreams*
                Hy Mayer
(21) Oct. 2   *Down to the Fair*

		Hy Mayer
(22)	Oct. 16	*Summer Scenes*
		Hy Mayer
(23)	Oct. 30	*All Aboard*
		Hy Mayer
(24)	Nov. 20	*New York*
		Hy Mayer
(25)	Dec.	*Puppies*
		Hy Mayer

1922

(26)	Oct. 14	*In the Dear Old Summer Time*
		Hy Mayer
(27)	Nov. 25	*Sporting Scenes*
		Hy Mayer

1923

(28)	Jan. 6	*Faces*
		Hy Mayer
(29)	March 24	*Silliettes*
		Herbert Dawley
(30)	April 7	*The Lobster Nightmare*
		Herbert Dawley
(31)	June 9	*The Absent Minded Poet*
		Herbert Dawley
(32)	July 7	*The Classic Centaur*
		Herbert Dawley

1924

(33)	Feb. 9	*Pan the Piper*
		Herbert Dawley
(34)	Aug. 9	*Fable of the Future: The Proxy Lover*
		Max Fleischer
(35)	Sept. 13	*The Makin's of an Artist*
		Hy Mayer
(36)	Sept. 27	*Thumbelina*
		Herbert Dawley
(37)		*Jack and the Beanstalk*
		Herbert Dawley
(38)		*Cinderella*
		Herbert Dawley

(39)   *Sleeping Beauty*
            Herbert Dawley
(40)   *Beauty and the Beast*
            Herbert Dawley
(41)   *Tattercoats*
            Herbert Dawley
(42)   *Aladdin and the Wonderful Lamp*
            Herbert Dawley

1925
(43)   March 28 (title untraced)
(44)   May 9   *Jack the Giant Killer*
                  Herbert Dawley
(45)   May 16   *The Making of a Man*
                  Hy Mayer

1926
(46)   Nov. 13   *Around the World in 28 Days*
                  Director: Bert Green

122. *Pen and Ink Vaudeville*

Earl Hurd Productions
Producer/Director/Story/Animation: Earl Hurd
Distributor: Educational Film Corp.

1924
(1)   Aug. 31   *Boneyard Blues*
(2)   Oct. 5   *The Hoboken Nightingale*
(3)   Nov. 2   *The Sawmill Four*
(4)   Nov. 15   *The Artist's Model*
(5)   Dec. 20   *Broadcasting*

1925
(6)   Feb. 7   *He Who Gets Socked*
(7)   March 7   *Two Cats and a Bird*
(8)   April 4   *The Mellow Quartette*
(9)   May 2   *Monkey Business*
(10)   May 30   *Two Poor Fish*
(11)   June 20   *Props' Dash for Cash*

(12)　July 4　　*Bobby Bumps and Co.*
(13)　Sept. 5　　*Props and the Spirits*

123. Dinky Doodle

GB: *Togo and Dinky*
Bray Productions
Producer: John R. Bray
Director/Story: Walter Lantz
Animation: Clyde Geronimi
Distributors: Standard Cinema Corp (1–2); Film Booking Offices
Combined live action and animation.

1924

(1)　Sept. 15　*The Magic Lamp*
　　　　　　　reissue: *Aladdin's Lamp*
(2)　Oct. 15　*The Giant Killer*
　　　　　　　reissue: *Jack and the Beanstalk*
(3)　Dec. 1　*The Pied Piper*

1925

(4)　Jan. 4　　*Little Red Riding Hood*
(5)　Feb. 1　　*The Captain's Kid*
　　　　　　　reissue: *Captain Kid*
(6)　Feb. 1　　*The House that Dinky Built*
(7)　March 1　*Cinderella*
(8)　April 26　*Peter Pan Handled*
(9)　May 24　*The Magic Carpet*
　　　　　　　reissue: *The Magic Rug*
(10)　June 21　*Robinson Crusoe*
(11)　July 19　*The Three Bears*
(12)　Aug. 16　*The Babes in the Woods*
(13)　Sept. 13　*Just Spooks*
(14)　Sept. 10　*Dinky Doodle and the Bad Man*
(15)　Nov. 1　*Dinky Doodle in the Hunt*
(16)　Nov. 29　*Dinky Doodle in the Circus*
(17)　Dec. 27　*Dinky Doodle in the Restaurant*

1926

(18)　Feb. 19　*Dinky Doodle in Lost and Found*

(19) Feb. 21 *Dinky Doodle in Uncle Tom's Cabin*
(20) March 21 *Dinky Doodle in the Arctic*
(21) April 8 *Dinky Doodle in Egypt*
(22) May 12 *Dinky Doodle in the Wild West*
(23) June 6 *Dinky Doodle's Bedtime Story*
reissue: *Bedtime Stories*
(24) July 4 *Dinky Doodle and the Little Orphan*
(25) July 24 *The Magician*
(26) Aug. 29 *Dinky Doodle in the Army*

124. *Animated Hair Cartoons*

Producer: Max Fleischer
Director/Story/Animation: "Marcus"
Distributor: Red Seal Pictures

1924

(1) Oct. 1 No. AA
(2) Nov. 22 No. BB

1925

(3) Feb. 2 No. CC
(4) March 2 No. DD
(5) April 2 No. EE
(6) April 9 No. FF
(7) April 16 No. GG
(8) April 25 No. HH
(9) May 9 No. II
(10) May 17 No. JJ
(11) May 24 No. KK
(12) May 30 No. LL
(13) June 6 No. MM
(14) June 13 No. NN
(15) June 20 No. OO
(16) June 27 No. PP
(17) July 4 No. QQ
(18) July 11 No. RR
(19) July 18 No. SS
(20) July 25 No. TT

(21)	Aug. 1	No. UU
(22)	Aug. 8	No. VV
(23)	Aug. 15	No. WW
(24)	Aug. 22	No. XX
(25)	Aug. 29	No. YY
(26)	Sept. 5	No. ZZ
(27)	Oct. 15	No. 1
(28)	Nov. 15	No. 2
(29)	Dec. 15	No. 3

1926

(30)	Jan. 15	No. 4
(31)	Feb. 15	No. 5
(32)	March 15	No. 6
(33)	April 10	No. 7
(34)	May 1	No. 8
(35)	June 12	No. 9
(36)	June 25	No. 10
(37)	July 17	No. 11
(38)	July 31	No. 12
(39)	Aug. 14	No. 13
(40)	Aug. 28	No. 14
(41)	Sept. 11	No. 15
(42)	Sept. 25	No. 16
(43)	Oct. 16	No. 17
(44)	Nov. 15	No. 18
(45)	Dec. 1	No. 19
(46)	Dec. 15	No. 20

1927

(47)	Jan. 1	No. 21
(48)	Jan. 15	No. 22
(49)	Feb. 15	No. 23
(50)	March 15	No. 24
(51)	April 15	No. 25

125. *Inklings*

GB: *Snip-Shots*

Red Seal Pictures
Producer: Max Fleischer
Director: Dave Fleischer
Series of miscellaneous short sequences featuring various types of
    animation: cut-outs, etc. Produced in 1924–1925, not released
    until November 1927–1928.
Released in GB in the 1930s with added soundtrack and commen-
    tary by New Realm Pictures.

1924–1925
Untitled series: numbered from 1 to 18.

126. *Animated Crosswords*

Banner Productions Inc.
Producer: C.H. Ferrell
Director/Story/Animation: Bert Green

1925
(1) Jan. 27   *Animated Crosswords No. 1*
            (NB: no further editions traced.)

127. *Judge's Crossword Puzzles*

GB: *Ideal Crossword Puzzles*
Crossword Film Company
Producer/Director/Animator: John Colman Terry
Distributor: Educational Pictures Corp.

1925
(1)   Jan. 31   No. 1
(2)   March 8   No. 2
(3)   March 15   No. 3
(4)   March 22   No. 4
(5)   March 29   No. 5
(6)   April 5   No. 6
(7)   April 12   No. 7
(8)   April 19   No. 8
(9)   April 26   No. 9
(10)   May 3   No. 10

128.   *Ebenezer Ebony*

Sering D. Wilson & Co.
Kelly Color

1925

(1)	April 22	*The Flying Elephant*
(2)	May 22	*An Ice Boy*
(3)	June 22	*Gypping the Gypsies*
(4)	July 1	*Fire in a Brimstone*
(5)	Aug. 1	*High Moon*
(6)	Sept. 1	*Love Honor and Oh Boy*
(7)	Oct. 1	*Foam Sweet Foam*
(8)	Oct. 31	*Fisherman's Luck*

129.   *Un-Natural History*

Bray Productions
Producer: John R. Bray
Directors: Walter Lantz, Clyde Geronimi
Animation: Walter Lantz, David Hand, Clyde Geronimi, Earl
    Hurd
Story: Walter Lantz, Joe Rock
Actors: Walter Lantz, Frankie Evans, Nancy Kelly
Distributor: Standard Cinema Corporation (1–3); Film Booking
    Offices (4–16)
Combined animation and live action.

1925

(1)	Oct. 4	*How the Elephant Got His Trunk*
		Director: Walter Lantz
(2)	Oct. 18	*How the Bear Got His Short Tail*
		Director: Walter Lantz
(3)	Nov. 15	*How the Camel Got His Hump*
		Director: Clyde Geronimi
		Animator: Earl Hurd
(4)	Dec. 13	*The Leopard's Spots*

1926

(5)	Jan. 10	*The Goat's Whiskers*
		Story: Joe Rock

(6)	Feb. 7	*How the Giraffe Got His Long Neck*
		reissue: *The Giraffe's Long Neck*
(7)	March 7	*The Stork Brought It*
(8)	April 4	*The King of the Beasts*
(9)	April 19	*The Ostrich's Plumes*
(10)	May 30	*The Pelican's Bill*
(11)	June 20	*The Cat's Whiskers*
(12)	July 18	*The Mule's Disposition*
(13)	Aug. 15	*The Pig's Curly Tail*
(14)	Dec. 29	*The Tail of the Monkey*
		reissue: *The Tale of the Monk*
		Director: Walter Lantz, David Hand

1927

(15)	Jan. 15	*The Cat's Nine Lives*
		Director/Story/Animator: Walter Lantz, David Hand, Clyde Geronimi
(16)	Jan. 18	*The Hyena's Laugh*
		Director/Story/Animator: Walter Lantz, Clyde Geronimi

130. *Little Ebony*

L.B. Cornwell Inc.

1925

(1)	Oct. 15	*Ebony Cleans Up*
(2)	Nov. 1	*The Stowaway*
(3)	Dec. 30	*A Drop in the Bucket*

1926
(NB: 23 further films in this series were released, titles untraced.)

131. *Colored Cartoon Comics*

Charles Bowers Cartoons
Distributor: Short Film Syndicate

1925
(Series of 26 cartoons: titles untraced.)

132. Popular Song Parodies

Artclass Pictures
Producer: Louis Weiss
Distributor: Film Booking Offices

1926

(1)	May	*Alexander's Ragtime Band*
(2)		*Annie Laurie*
(3)		*The Sheik of Araby*
(4)		*In My Harem*
(5)		*When I Lost You*
(6)		*Margie*
(7)		*When that Midnight Choochoo Leaves for Alabam*
(8)		*Oh What a Pal Was Mary*
(9)		*Everybody's Doing It*
(10)		*My Wife's Gone to the Country*
(11)		*Oh How I Hate to Get Up in the Morning*
(12)		*Just Try to Picture Me*
(13)		*I Love to Fall Asleep*
(14)		*For Me and My Gal*
(15)		*Yak-a-Hula-Hick-a-Doola*
(16)		*My Sweetie*
(17)		*Old Pal*
(18)		*Tumbledown Shack in Athlone*
(19)		*The Rocky Road to Dublin*
(20)		*When I Leave This World Behind*
(21)		*Finiculee Finicula*
(22)		*When the Angelus Was Ringing*
(23)		*Beautiful Eyes*
(24)		*Call Me Up Some Rainy Afternoon*
(25)		*Micky*
(26)		*Oh I Wish I Was in Michigan*

133. Scenic Sketchographs

Mayer
Producer/Director/Story/Animation: Henry (Hy) Mayer
Distributor: Pathé

1926

  (1) July 26   *The Family Album*
  (2) July 26   *Tripping the Rhine*
  (3) July 26   *A Pup's Tale*
  (4) July 26   *Nurenberg the Toy City*

134. *Life Cartoon Comedies*

Sherwood-Wadsworth Pictures
Distributor: Educational Pictures

1926

  (1) Sept. 18 *Red Hot Rails*
  (2) Sept. 25 *Flaming Ice*
  (3) Sept. 25 *Missing Links*
  (4) Oct. 5   *The Yellow Pirate*
  (5) Oct. 11 *Cut Price Glory*
  (6) Nov. 7   *The Mighty Smithy*
  (7) Nov. 21 *Barnum Was Right*
  (8) Dec. 5   *Balloon Tired*
  (9) Dec. 16 *Why Women Pay*

1927

  (10) Jan. 2   *The Peaceful City*
  (11) Jan. 18 *Mike Wins a Medal*
  (12) Jan. 30 *Soft Soap*
  (13) Feb. 8   *A Heavy Date*
  (14) Feb. 23 *Hitting the Trail*
  (15) March 8 *Local Talent*
  (16) March 27 *Ruling the Rooster*
  (17) April 10 *The Prince of Whales*
  (18) April 24 *Racing Fever*
  (19) May 8   *North of Nowhere*

135. *Hot Dog Cartoons*

Bray Productions
Producer: John R. Bray
Directors: Walter Lantz, Clyde Geronimi

1926

- **(1)** Oct. 2   *For the Love o' Pete*
- **(2)** Oct. 5   *Pete's Haunted House*
- **(3)** Oct. 26   *Pete's Party*

1927

- **(4)** Jan. 4   *Dog Gone It*
- **(5)** Jan. 31   *Along Came Fido*
- **(6)** Feb. 4   *The Puppy Express*
- **(7)** Feb. 16   *Petering Out*
- **(8)** March 15 *S'Matter Pete*
- **(9)** April 8   *Pete's Pow-Wow*
- **(10)** April 8   *Lunch Hound*
- **(11)** April 26 *Jingle Bells*
- **(12)** May 14   *Bone Dry*
- **(13)** May 27   *The Farm Hand*

136.   Camera Mysteries

GB: *Screen Revelations*
Swartz Pictures
Producer: George D. Swartz
Director/Story/Animation: Luis Seel

1926

- **(1)**   *Finding the Lost World*
- **(2)**   *Rushing the Gold Rush*
- **(3)**   *The Flying Carpet*
- **(4)**   *Safety Not Last*
- **(5)**   *Motoring*
- **(6)**   *Pirates Bold*

137.   Oswald the Lucky Rabbit

Winkler Productions
Producer: Charles Mintz
Director: Walt Disney
Animation: Ubbe Iwerks, Walter Lantz, Hugh Harman, Walker

Harman, Rudolf Ising, Isadore Freleng, Rollin Hamilton, Ben
Clopton, Carman Maxwell
Distributor: Universal "Snappy"

1927

(1)	June 9	*Trolley Troubles*
		reissue with sound: 11.23.31
(2)	July 20	*Oh Teacher*
		reissue with sound: 2.1.32
(3)	Sept. 8	*The Ocean Hop*
		reissue with sound: 4.24.32
(4)	Sept. 10	*All Wet*
		reissue with sound: 2.1.32
(5)	Sept. 10	*The Mechanical Cow*
(6)	Sept. 15	*The Banker's Daughter*
(7)	Sept. 15	*Great Guns*
		reissue with sound: 2.29.32
(8)	Oct. 19	*Rickety Gin*
(9)	Nov. 23	*Empty Socks*
(10)	Dec. 20	*Harem Scarem*
(11)	Dec. 28	*Neck 'n' Neck*

1928

(12)	Jan. 17	*The Ole Swimmin' Hole*
(13)	Feb. 3	*Africa Before Dark*
(14)	Feb. 16	*Rival Romeos*
(15)	March 1	*Bright Lights*
(16)	March 14	*Sagebrush Sadie*
(17)	March 29	*Ozzie of the Mounted*
(18)	March 29	*Ride 'Em Plowboy*
(19)	March 30	*Oh What a Knight*
(20)	March 30	*Hungry Hoboes*
(21)	April 25	*Sky Scrappers*
(22)	May 22	*Poor Papa*
(23)	June 6	*The Fox Chase*
(24)	June 20	*Tall Timber*
(25)	July 3	*Sleigh Bells*
(26)	Aug. 3	*Hot Dog*
		(Last Walt Disney "Oswald.")

(27) July 23   *High Up*
              Director: Rudolf Ising, Rollin Hamilton
(28) Aug. 17   *Panicky Pancakes*
              Director: Hugh Harman, Ben Clopton
(29) Aug. 30   *Mississippi Mud*
              Director: Walter Lantz
(30) Sept. 27 *Fiery Fireman*
              Director: Rudolf Ising, Isadore Freleng
(31) Oct. 2   *The South Pole Flight*
              Director: Hugh Harman, Ben Clopton
(32) Oct. 11   *Bull-Oney*
              Director: Walter Lantz, Tom Palmer
(33) Oct. 24   *Rocks and Socks*
              Director: Hugh Harman
(34) Nov. 12   *Homeless Homer*
              Director: Rudolf Ising, Isadore Freleng
(35) Nov. 14   *Farmyard Follies*
              Director: Walter Lantz, Rollin Hamilton
(36) Nov. 19   *A Horse Tale*
              Director: Rollin Hamilton, Tom Palmer
(37) Dec. 26   *Yanky Clippers*
              Director: Walter Lantz, Tom Palmer
(Last silent "Oswald" cartoon. Series continued with soundtrack.)

138. *The Inkwell Imps*

(Continuation of *Out of the Inkwell* series.)
Out of the Inkwell Films
Producers: Max Fleischer, Alfred Weiss
Director: Dave Fleischer
Animators: Dick Huemer, Roland Crandall
Distributor: Paramount Famous Lasky Corporation

1927
(1) Aug. 6   *Koko Plays Pool*
(2) Aug. 20   *Koko's Kane*
(3) Sept. 3   *Koko the Knight*
(4) Sept. 17 *Koko Hops Off*
(5) Oct. 1   *Koko the Kop*

(6)   Oct. 15   *Koko Explores*
(7)   Oct. 29   *Koko Chops Suey*
(8)   Nov. 12   *Koko's Klock*
(9)   Nov. 26   *Koko Kicks*
(10) Dec. 10   *Koko's Quest*
(11) Dec. 24   *Koko the Kid*

1928
(12) Jan. 7   *Koko's Kink*
(13) Jan. 21   *Koko's Kozy Korner*
(14) Feb. 4   *Koko's Germ Jam*
(15) Feb. 18   *Koko's Bawth*
(16) March 3   *Koko Smokes*
(17) March 17   *Koko's Tattoo*
(18) March 31   *Koko's Earth Control*
(19) April 14   *Koko's Hot Dog*
(20) April 28   *Koko's Haunted House*
(21) May 12   *Koko Lamps Aladdin*
(22) May 26   *Koko Squeals*
(23) June 9   *Koko's Field Daze*
(24) June 23   *Koko Goes Over*
(25) July 7   *Koko's Catch*
(26) July 21   *Koko's War Dogs*
(27) Aug. 11   *Koko's Chase*
(28) Aug. 25   *Koko Heaves Ho*
(29) Sept. 7   *Koko's Big Pull*
(30) Sept. 21   *Koko Cleans Up*
(31) Oct. 8   *Koko's Parade*
(32) Oct. 22   *Koko's Dog Gone*
(33) Nov. 3   *Koko in the Rough*
(34) Nov. 8   *After the Ball*
(35) Nov. 16   *Koko's Magic*
(36) Dec. 4   *Koko on the Track*
(37) Dec. 17   *Koko's Act*
(38) Dec. 28   *Koko's Courtship*

1929
(39) Jan. 11   *No Eyes Today*
(40) Jan. 25   *Noise Annoys Koko*

(41)	Feb. 8	*Koko Beats Time*
(42)	Feb. 23	*Koko's Reward*
(43)	March 8	*Koko's Hot Ink*
(44)	March 23	*Koko's Crib*
(45)	April 5	*Koko's Saxaphonies*
(46)	April 19	*Koko's Knock-down*
(47)	May 3	*Koko's Signals*
(48)	May 17	*Koko's Focus*
(49)	May 31	*Koko's Conquest*
(50)	June 14	*Koko's Harem Scarem*
(51)	June 28	*Koko's Big Sale*
(52)	July 12	*Koko's Hypnotism*
(53)	July 26	*Chemical Koko*

139. *Newslaffs*

Film Booking Offices
Producer/Director/Story/Animation: William C. Nolan

1927

(1)	Sept. 4	No. 1
(2)	Sept. 18	No. 2
(3)	Oct. 2	No. 3
(4)	Oct. 16	No. 4
(5)	Oct. 30	No. 5
(6)	Nov. 13	No. 6
(7)	Nov. 27	No. 7
(8)	Dec. 11	No. 8
(9)	Dec. 25	No. 9

1928

(10)	Jan. 8	No. 10
(11)	Jan.	No. 11
(12)	Feb. 5	No. 12
(13)	Feb. 19	No. 13
(14)	March 2	No. 14
(15)	March 2	No. 15
(16)	March 5	No. 16
(17)	April 16	No. 17

(18)	April 30	No. 18
(19)	May 14	No. 19
(20)	May 28	No. 20
(21)	June 11	No. 21
(22)	June 25	No. 22
(23)	July 9	No. 23
(24)	July 23	No. 24

140. *Mickey Mouse*

Walt Disney Comic
Producer: Walter Elias Disney
Director: Ubbe Iwerks
Animation: Wilfred Jackson, Ubbe Iwerks, Les Clark, John Cannon, Ben Sharpsteen, Burton Gillett, Jack King, Norman Ferguson
Distributor: Celebrity Productions

1928

(1) May 15 *Plane Crazy*
      Director: Ubbe Iwerks
      (*NB*: Not released as a silent film. Sound added for release 5.1929)

(2) Aug. 7 *The Gallopin' Goucho*
      Director: Ubbe Iwerks
      (NB: Not released as a silent film. Sound added for release 5.1929)

Name Index

Numbers refer to entry numbers, not page numbers.

163

Title Index

Numbers refer to entry numbers, not page numbers. Numbers in parentheses are sub-entry numbers. Series titles are in **boldface** type.

A

Abie Kabibble Outwitting His Rival 73 (2)
Abie the Agent 73
Abraham and the Opossum 49 (32)
The Absent Minded Poet 114 (3), 121 (31)
Absent Minded Willie 49 (48)
The Accident Attorney 8 (84)
Accidents Will Happen 97 (16)
Accidents Won't Happen 8 (293)
An Ace and a Joker 8 (81)
The Adventures of Adenoid 102 (200)
The Adventures of Hardrock Dome 64 (113)
The Adventures of Hardrock Dome No. 2 64 (114)
Adventures of Mr. Common People 63 (8)
The Adventures of Mr. Phiffles 9 (13)
Adventures of Roving Thomas 110
The Adventures of Tom the Tamer and Kid Kelly 23 (14)

Aerial Warfare 64 (91)
Aero Nuts 45 (88)
The Aeroplane Machine Gun 64 (46)
Aesop's Film Fables 102
Africa Before Dark 137 (13)
An African Hunt 13 (13)
African Huntsmen 102 (187)
After the Ball 57 (37), 138 (34)
Aged in the Wood 102 (121)
A-Hunting We Will Go 97 (38)
Air Cooled 102 (227)
Aladdin and the Wonderful Lamp 114 (12), 121 (42)
Aladdin's Lamp 123 (1)
Alaska or Bust 102 (375)
Alexander's Ragtime Band 132 (1)
Alice and the Dog Catcher 118 (6)
Alice and the Three Bears 118 (10)
Alice at the Carnival 118 (44)
Alice at the Rodeo 118 (45)
Alice Cans the Cannibals 118 (12)
Alice Charms the Fish 118 (32)
Alice Chops the Suey 118 (24)
Alice Comedies 118
Alice Cuts the Ice 118 (37)

The Ball Game 8 (21)
The Ball Park 102 (406)
Balloon Tired 134 (8)
Balloons 78 (38)
Bang Go the Rifles 36 (8), 41 (1)
The Banker's Daughter 137 (6)
The Bare Idea 8 (195)
Barnum Was Right 134 (7)
Barnyard Artists 102 (357)
Barnyard Follies 102 (221)
A Barnyard Hamlet 17 (58)
Barnyard Lodge Number One
   102 (355)
A Barnyard Mixup 13 (12)
A Barnyard Nightmare 17 (44)
The Barnyard Olympics 102 (167)
Barnyard Politics 102 (385)
A Barnyard Rodeo 102 (124)
Baron Bragg and the Devilish
   Dragon 103 (14)
Baron Bragg and the Haunted
   Castle 103 (16)
Bars and Stripes 102 (288)
Baseball 8 (18), 121 (4)
The Bath 6 (35)
The Battle 78 (36)
A Battling Duet 102 (356)
Battling for Barleycorn 45 (48)
Beaches and Scream 45 (115)
The Bear and the Bees 102 (31)
The Bear Facts 8 (297)
Bear Facts 80 (27)
The Bearded Lady 8 (107)
Beaten by a Hare 59 (29), 86
   (70)
Beautiful Eyes 132 (23)
The Beautiful Model 8 (179)
Beauty and the Beach 105 (14)
Beauty and the Beast 114 (10),
   121 (40)
The Beauty Parlour 102 (106)
Bed Time 78 (41)
Bedtime Stories 123 (23)
Bee Cause 45 (83)
Behind the Scenes of the Circus
   30 (21)

Behind the Signs of Broadway 86
   (22)
The Bell Hops 8 (52)
The Berth of a Nation 8 (163)
Bertlevyettes 18
Beside the Cider 8 (263)
The Best Man Loses 61 (32)
The Best Man Wins 102 (129)
The Best Mouse Loses 45 (29),
   86 (32)
The Best of Luck 97 (40)
Best Wishes 45 (78)
The Bicycle Race 8 (181)
The Big Burg 102 (399)
Big Chief Koko 78 (57)
The Big Flood 102 (68)
The Big Game 102 (380)
The Big-hearted Fish 102 (252)
The Big Retreat 102 (259)
The Big Reward 102 (316)
The Big Scare 102 (426)
The Big Shot 102 (402)
The Big Show 105 (17)
The Big Swim 8 (311)
The Big Tent 102 (333)
Bigger and Better Jails 102 (191)
Billy Sunday's Tabernacle 63 (5)
The Biography of Madame
   Fashion 64 (132)
A Bird of Flight 111 (55)
The Birth of the Trick Kids 47 (1)
The Birthday 78 (30)
Biting the Dust 102 (189)
Black and White 45 (79)
The Black Duck 102 (397)
The Black Fist 61 (28)
The Black List 21 (34)
Black Magic 98 (14), 101 (17),
   102 (174)
The Black Sheep 102 (136)
Black Sunlight 112 (6)
Black's Mysterious Box 23 (13)
Blackman Cartoons 1
Blackton Cartoons 1
A Blaze of Glory 102 (349)
The Boarding House 8 (54)

The Hole Cheese 8 (266)
A Hole in One 102 (325)
The Home Agent 102 (343)
Home Brew 8 (213)
Home Sweet Home 8 (202), 52 (6), 102 (280)
Home Talent 102 (158)
Homeless Cats 102 (404)
Homeless Homer 137 (34)
Homeless Pups 102 (150)
The Honest Book Agent 8 (141)
The Honest Jockey 8 (180)
The Honor Man 102 (305)
The Honor System 102 (230)
The Hooch Ball 80 (23)
Hook, Line and Sinker 102 (326)
Hoot Mon 8 (274)
Hootch and Mootch in a Steak at Stake 90 (50)
Hop, Skip and Jump 8 (279)
Horse Play 45 (65)
Horse Tail 137 (36)
Horses, Horses, Horses 102 (311)
A Horse's Tale 102 (344)
Hospital Orderlies 8 (72)
Hospitalities 45 (121)
Hot Dog 137 (26)
Hot Dog Cartoons 135
Hot Dogs 8 (198), 45 (39)
Hot Shots 111 (4)
A Hot Time in Punkville 13 (9)
A Hot Time in the Gym 60 (4)
Hot Times in Iceland 102 (207)
Hotel de Mutt 8 (79)
House Cleaning 102 (166), (203)
The House in Which They Live 46 (5)
The House That Dinky Built 123 (6)
The Housing Shortage 102 (198)
How a Mosquito Operates 3 (2)
How Animated Cartoons Are Made 86 (2)
How Charlie Captured the Kaiser 81 (1)
How Could William Tell 59

(10), 86 (14)
How Dizzy Joe Got to Heaven 38 (9)
How I Became Crazy 45 (35)
How I Became Krazy 86 (83)
How It Feels 30 (34)
How Many Bars in a Beetle's Beat 68 (14)
How My Vacation Spent Me 86 (52), 96 (2)
How the Bear Got His Short Tail 129 (2)
How the Camel Got His Hump 129 (3)
How the Elephant Got His Trunk 129 (1)
How the Giraffe Got His Long Neck 129 (6)
How to Please the Public 111 (66)
How Troy Was Collared 117 (10)
How You See 86 (29)
Howdy Partner 97 (29)
The Hula-Hula Cabaret 8 (104)
Hula-Hula Town 8 (178)
The Human Fly 102 (329)
Humorous Cartoon 1 (1)
Humorous Phases of Funny Faces 2 (2)
Humors of Summer 9 (17)
A Hunger Stroke 45 (98)
Hungry Hoboes 137 (20)
Hungry Hounds 102 (223)
The Hungry Mosquito 3 (2)
The Hunter and His Dog 102 (49)
A Hunting Absurdity 13 (5)
Hunting Big Game 93 (5), 95 (25)
Hunting in Crazyland 17 (1)
Hunting in 1950 102 (245)
Hunting the U-Boats 8 (78)
The Huntsman 102 (366)
Hy Mayer Cartoons 9
Hy Mayer Cartoons 9 (18), 68
Hy Mayer His Magic Hand 9 (2)

Y

Z